He's Not Your Girlfriend

How to understand men in love and thrive in your relationship

He's Not Your Girlfriend

How to understand men in love and thrive in your relationship

Carolyn Casey

Book cover design by Red Boots Creative

To My Love—
You are right: we make the best team!
Thank you for picking me—best decision I've ever made.
You love me so well every day, and I am forever grateful.

To My Girl—
May you live your own fabulous love story.

Acknowledgements

I have found that every great accomplishment in my life has been supported by a cast of characters, many of whom helped me on multiple occasions in my life. This book is no exception.

My two biggest cheerleaders are my mom and my husband. They pick me up, dust me off and send me out into the world with so much love. My daughter has had fewer years in the game, though she is equally adamant that I can do anything. Tears well up and I am overcome with emotion as I contemplate their fervent love and their belief in me. It is very meaningful and often needed. Thank you!

My husband, Clint, gets extra credit in this book as he has been my rock through the many years of my journey to understand male and female dynamics, initially with the diversity work I did in the corporate world, then through years of consulting, speaking, workshop development and training work I did for Delia Passi, founder of Women Certified. And finally, in this last phase, Clint has lived the culmination of pulling it all together around romantic relationships.

Clint is a man who prefers to remain private. Yet in supporting me, he has attended seminars, he's been my teaching partner in relationship workshops I have led, and he's been experimented on more than most men on the planet. Thank you for your willingness to do whatever it takes (including allow me to share our stories in this book).

This journey to deeper understanding of men and women in relationships started with a Magical Relationships workshop taught by Eva Love and Will Noyes, who were the sparks that lit my fire. What an eye opener for me and a transformer of Clint's and my love life! Following that monumental event, they gave a workshop in our hometown for our friends and family. Later, Eva and Will met with us as we developed our own workshop content. They graciously allowed us to rely upon much of their knowledge as a starting point. Eva and Will are masters at what they do, and I remain grateful for the new perspective they helped me discover regarding what is possible between men and women in love.

Last, but certainly not least, I want to acknowledge my girlfriends along the journey. You know who you are. You are the ones I call when I need reminding that all is possible in life and that a miracle is on the way. You are the ones who have shared my delight in how the universe has unfolded the latest "Aha!" in my life. You are the ones who have reminded me to ask for help and that there is always more happening than meets the eye. You are my village of hope and inspiration, my living angels, and I am grateful.

Contents

Part II: Living The Differences

He Loves To Deliver (When He Wins)   53

He Won't Lead At Intimacy   64

He Won't Win At "House" (Unless You Let Him)   70

He's Not Broken   79

Part III: Reality Check!

Part IV: Everyone Wins

Introduction

Relationships are meant to be fun and uplifting. Both women and men agree on this fundamental notion. Unfortunately, it is easy to lose track of this simple idea. At the exciting start of a relationship, it is easier to be clear on this viewpoint. Men and women live the excitement together—what fun! But too often life's details get in the way:

- Demanding work schedules
- A home with all of its upkeep
- Kids—and all of their upkeep!
- Double sets of family members (parents, grandparents, etc.)—and all of their emotional upkeep

Gradually, we can move from a carefree, whirlwind love affair to a transactional, "who's-doing-what-when" efficiency relationship. What happened to the fun? That's where this book comes in. The ideas and tools in this book can help you reclaim that uplifting love relationship and keep it going. What's your current relationship status?

Single and want a fabulous relationship—Allow this book to reset your vision for your future relationship. Use it to learn from past experiences and reset your beliefs about what is possible in romance.

Married or in a committed relationship you would describe as "ho-hum" (or worse) —The ideas and simple tools presented here can revive and revitalize you and your relationship.

Good-to-Great—If you and your partner have a really good relationship (and are perhaps admired by many as an ideal couple), I can relate. That's where my husband, Clint, and I were when many of these ideas were first introduced to me: 15 years happily and successfully married. Here's the truly great part—there's more to enjoy! You and your partner can learn to *thrive* with each other and grow together. You can take what is already "good-to-great" and make it "great-to-thriving."

Wherever your starting point, I believe with all of my heart there's something here for you. You may gain a new perspective. You may find a new pointer or approach. Sometimes a simple new idea unlocks a flood of new experiences. This has been the case with all of the relationship workshops I've taught and the couples I've encountered.

It is my great honor and joy to share new perspectives and life-changing ways of being in relationship. Keep your mind and heart open.

Carolyn Casey
Boise, Idaho
March 2013

Three Ways To Read This Book

For The Most Enjoyment, Do It Your Way!

There are a million ways to do anything, including how to read a book. This book is no exception. I want to make sure that I remove any guilt from your reading right from the start. (With this book's title, do you really think there is a guilt trip here?) It is perfectly okay to read different sections differently. Trust that however you are reading this book is right for you at this time. You can always re-read or skim again later.

Breeze Through (light approach)

Breeze through the book to get to the end so you know the gist of what is in it. As Edi Spanier says, "Once you know, you can't not know." Thus, you have created value by planting seeds to germinate in your mind about relationship possibilities.

Stop 'N Shop (medium approach)

Read a bit. Stop to contemplate. Perhaps test out a tool or two. Bring up an idea with a friend to discuss and weigh the merits. Honestly, if you only find one thing to do differently, you'll change your relationship for the better.

Devour (deep approach)

Devour the book. Please do! Experience every exercise. Use every tool. Drive others crazy quoting it and the perspective it offers. Change your love life dramatically.

A Note To Readers

There are three things to know while reading this book:

1. Throughout this book, I comment on differences between men and women. The truth is we all have both male and female traits. Whenever I speak to groups or do trainings, I begin by saying "Generally speaking and *always* with exceptions." That same truth applies here. Rather than spending your reading time thinking of the exceptions, find the truth in the situation for you, regardless of your gender. To help readers in this regard, I have shared areas where I have more male tendencies.

2. I am not a psychologist, psychiatrist or a relationship or marriage counselor. My work is focused on helping emotionally healthy men and women in their relationships. In all cases throughout this book, I am speaking about emotionally healthy men. An emotionally healthy man is one who is motivated to please the woman in his life, to make her happy. He is a man who wants to "win" with her. He is a man who responds well to her acknowledgement and gratitude— he smiles or even physically stands taller when he receives her compliments. (I say, "He puffs up.") He may also repeat the behaviors she likes.

3. All of the names used in the examples, with the exception of my husband's and mine, have been changed. Further, any identifying information was also altered. This allows my clients to share their relationship journey with me knowing it is received with respect and treated confidentially.

Part I

Living Our Differences

He Didn't Play With Dolls

I believe that how boys grow up playing is the crux of how men show up in their romantic relationships. Since it's that important, it bears exploring. Stop and think about what you played as a child. Mentally, make a list of a few games or things you played with as a child. Reflect and contrast your experience to what your siblings played (if you had them) or what your children or nieces/nephews have played. Perhaps you were like me growing up with brothers, so you were a tomboy. You didn't play the traditional things that girls do, like dolls and Barbies. Or, perhaps you were a boy who had sisters. Did your sisters play dress up or dolls? Did you play with them? The truth is, even the exceptions to typical play hardly matter. What is important is the *way* that boys and girls play is different. The way we play is unique to each gender.

That boys and girls play differently is likely not news to you. This is something we've all known about boys and girls since we were quite young. This is why at various points throughout their adolescence, girls play with girls and boys play with boys. Not only do we play differently, we typically play different games and with different toys. Most of us haven't stopped to think about this fundamental difference. I certainly hadn't. What I know now is this one idea helps explain why men and women behave differently in our relationships and, ultimately, in our marriages.

I ask the question about how people played as children to every audience I speak to or in every workshop I teach.

Invariably, I hear the men played the range of sports: football, baseball, basketball, etc. They also rode bicycles and played super heroes, cops & robbers or Army. As you might imagine, I have never heard a man shouting out that he played with dolls. That wouldn't go over well in a crowd with other men, and there's good reason for it, which I address later. The women played house, doctor, dress up and all varieties of doll games. They also played various sports, like volleyball, soccer, softball, basketball, etc.

Before I go any deeper, I want to revisit one of the points I put in the **A Note To Readers** section, in case you are the type of reader who skips over the first part of books. Throughout this book I am referring to basic generalities about men and women. The truth is, we all have both male and female traits. Whenever I speak to groups or do trainings, I begin by saying "Generally speaking and *always* with exceptions." That same truth applies here. Rather than spending your reading time thinking of the exceptions, find the truth in the situation for you, regardless of your gender. A woman in one of my relationship workshops was convinced that everything I said about men described her in her relationship and conversely everything I said about women more aptly described her husband. Even if that is the case for you, the perspective, ideas and tools I share will reshape the way you experience your relationship and allow you to create more understanding and joy—more delight—with one another.

Boys Play Competition

When boys play, there is always an element of competition. They make a competition out of *everything*. If they are riding bikes, the competition becomes who can go the fastest, jump the highest off the curb or ride a wheelie the farthest. Even if they are spitting, the game becomes who has the biggest spit, who can spit the farthest or who is the most precise in hitting something with his spit. This scenario also holds true for throwing rocks, snowballs or anything that can be launched.

If you are a woman who didn't grow up around boys, ask some of the men in your life what they played growing up. Then ask them if they kept score. When I ask audiences this, the men look at me as if I've come from another planet. I get looks that range from "She's an idiot!" to "Of course!" The score is always kept in the boy world.

Boys Always Want to Win

The reason boys keep score when they are playing is that they *always* want to win. Winning matters in the boy world. When boys play, it's not personal. They want to win, regardless of whom they are competing against, even if they are competing with their best friend. What is even better is to beat their best friend. For fun, and to make a point to the women, I ask the men in the audience if they wanted to win. Again, I get the looks as if I may not be a competent on the topic of boys and men after all. Recently I had one man say, "Still do [want to win]!" It was such a perfect response that I had him assure the audience that he didn't know me and wasn't a plant I had put in the audience to make my point.

How does the desire to win translate to your relationship? When boys grow up into emotionally healthy men, they most

9

want to "win" with the women in their lives. What winning with his woman means is not about sex; I am talking about pleasing her in all sorts of ways in her life. He wins with her when she acknowledges his actions with her joy and her gratitude.

The One-Upmanship Game

When boys win, often times they rub it in their friend's face for days, weeks, months or however long they have the bragging rights to do so. Winning is a big deal and it lives on long after the event. That is just how it works in the boy world. This is not a secret. You can ask men about this and they will tell you flat out that winning is paramount. A boy wants to win against his best friend, his brother, his cousin—everyone. And he wants to win at anything they do together. When a boy wins, he holds onto that win for as long as possible. If you know any men who continue to play sports like golf or tennis, or even casual sports like driveway basketball, you can witness this winning desire and one-upmanship. Pay attention to what happens during the game and then after the game is over. Listen in at the next reunion of friends, as the guys are hanging out swapping stories. You may hear bragging about a big sporting event from years earlier.

Another form of one-upmanship is ribbing. Ribbing is a sign of friendship that takes place amongst boys and men who are friends. Ribbing can also occur even if they are not friends. This is teasing, or banter, that goes back and forth between men. In my family when my brothers did this my mom called it "the cut-down game." My mom didn't like it, and my dad saw nothing wrong with it. Here's how it works. (This explanation is for the women readers as the men are fully aware of how this works.) First, a smart remark is launched from one guy to another, suggesting the "launcher's" superiority. It's generally a good-natured comment that is meant to put the "receiver" in his place, one notch below the launcher. It's a personal comment, only it's not taken personally. If the comment is taken personally, it is never publicly admitted, as that would add fuel to the ribbing fire. Then, the receiving guy responds with his own put-down remark. These comments can go back and forth endlessly. Surprisingly, ribbing comments from previous conversations can even pick up again after a long gap in seeing or being with each other. Ribbing is the reason that no man in a crowded room of men or women would openly admit to playing with dolls. The simple reason is it would give the other men too much ammunition to use against him at some point in the future.

I grew up around two brothers constantly ribbing each other, so I learned to give and receive ribbing. It became a form of play between us as siblings. Quite regularly I have heard a pair of men engaged in ribbing each other when I am training or facilitating in corporate meetings. If either of the men reminds me of my brother, I'm in trouble, as I often join in. This is not typical for a woman. (Nor, I realize, is it the best introduction to a facilitator or speaker.) What men know is that women typically don't engage in this type of banter, and I have discovered the banter dies down or the turns more gentle when a woman is present.

I have even played this ribbing game with my girlfriend Sally, who grew up with brothers, because she knows how to play too. Once, though, there was another woman, Carrie, present and we included her in our play (a very girl thing to do). Before long it was clear her feelings were hurt. She had grown up with a sister and even though she was married, she had no idea that Sally and I were playing a game. Up to this point Carrie hadn't noticed this prevalent behavior in the male world. As a result, she took our comments literally and personally. While common for men, ribbing is not a game well suited for the way girls and women are used to being in relationship with each other.

Girls Play Relationship

Girls are a different story. I typically get a broader range of responses about what girls played growing up. In addition to Barbies and playing house or dress up, girls have also played sports. (Thank you Title IX for making sports widely accessible to girls.) What's interesting to notice is that regardless of what girls are playing, there is an element of "relationship" to their play. This dynamic is obvious in a game where one girl is playing the teacher and the other girls are playing the students. It's obvious in all of the games girls play: house, Barbies or any other of the more traditional girl games. Even when girls play stuffed animals, as our daughter did, there is an element of one animal relating to another. It mystified my husband why our daughter would tell him exactly what his stuffed animal was supposed to do and say. Frankly, he didn't understand the game he was really playing with her. My husband thought he was engaged in imaginative play and thus he could do or say anything he wanted with his animal. Clearly he was playing a relationship game with our daughter. Our daughter continued imaginative play with him only as long as he remained within the bounds of girl culture relationship norms. Otherwise, he was to do with his stuffed animal as she instructed.

Even on highly competitive sports teams, girls add successful relationships with other teammates to the desire to win. I grew up playing basketball on an undefeated high school team (56-0 when I graduated) and then went on to play in college. I played quite competitively and obviously cared about winning. Still, it mattered to all of the girls on the team how we played together—the relationship dynamics among the players was at the core of the game. I recall the day our male coach was upset with our starting point guard, Terri, and had her move to the second string. What made this so horrifying to all of us is that he replaced her with her best friend, Leslie. "How can he do that?" we all wondered. The coach had disrupted a critical girl relationship and didn't even know it. He just thought he was doing the best thing for the team to win.

Audiences prove this point about how girls play competitive sports best for me. I give the following scenario to both the men and the women, always starting with the men. Whatever sport a man in the audience said he played growing up, say basketball, I let him know that he is forming a team and there's this guy who has an amazing shot from the outside. As they say in the lingo, "He's money." Then I qualify the player by letting the man know that the only problem with this player with the great shot is that "he is a jerk that nobody can stand." Then I ask, "Would you put him on your team?"

"Absolutely!" he answers. The other men in the room are nodding their heads in complete agreement, sometimes vigorously. This happens 99.99% of the time. Then I give one of the female athletes in the room the same scenario, adjusting only for the sport: she's forming a softball team and there is a girl who can hit a homerun every time. The problem is, "she's a jerk and nobody likes her." I ask, "Do you want her on your team?"

Ninety plus percent of the time the answer is a resounding, "No!" The other women in the room are often nodding vigorously in agreement. At this point the men are mystified. I ask the woman, "Don't you want to win?" Yes, all of the women I've asked say they want to win. The men are still very confused about what is going on with the women in this scenario, so I probe.

"You say you want to win and yet this woman hits a homerun every time and you don't want her on your team?"

"Right." I have to continue to ask the women in the room to explain because the men are dumbfounded by this. They honestly don't get it. Okay, every now and again there is a man present who does get it, but it's rare, and he is definitely the Lone Ranger in the room. I've done this with small groups of 25 and groups over 1,000 in size and the answer is always the same. The women explain, "It's not worth it. I want to win and I don't need to put up with her to win." In other words, women want to win on an athletic level and on a relationship level. Translation: I want my cake and I want to eat it too, thank you very much!

This is eye opening for both women and men. Women get to see how important winning is to men. They also see that men really don't care about relationship dynamics when it comes to winning. On the other hand, men see how important relationship dynamics are to women and that women would pass over a star player who is a jerk. Men also see that women are just as competitive-minded as men are and want to win, yet they are not willing to have potentially challenging or damaging relationship dynamics in the process. If you have a chance in a group of men and women, do this experiment yourself. It's fascinating.

For Girls Everything Is Personal

In the female culture everything—even competition—is personal. Girls, and then women, are forever navigating the waters of how to play relationship dynamics in everything they do. You can see this from the time girls are quite young. The next time you have the opportunity to experience a group of young girls, take a moment to listen in on their play conversation. Each girl is considering every other girl's feelings. And when there isn't consideration for each other's feeling, there are hurt feelings. As our daughter was growing up my husband was privy to her conversations about what happened amongst her girlfriends. Often he'd look at me, exasperated, and say, "Can't they all just get along and play?"

That is exactly what they did in his boy world. They played. You got beat today; you played the next day as usual. You were shoved by one guy; you resolved to beat him the next day. The game wasn't fair; you played and planned to win the next day. It wasn't *personal*. Or if it did feel personal, the antidote was to win the next time. Winning solves *everything* for a man.

He's Not Your Girlfriend

We already know that men and women are different. I am

suggesting you accept *how* men and women are different. Not good or bad, right or wrong. When we were young children we accepted the differences in how we played, not knowing that our play dynamics would set up how we behaved later in our relationships. Yet when it comes time to be in a relationship together, it is as if we have all gotten amnesia about the basic fact that we have differences that go beyond the physical differences. To be honest, the women seem to have the stronger cases of amnesia. Men, bless their hearts, are typically crystal clear that they are different from us and that they don't understand women.

I became shockingly aware of the genesis of the female version of amnesia while facilitating a relationship session at my annual mother-daughter camp, called U & Me Camp. This camp is for Moms and their teen/tween girls and is designed to create a strong bond to get them through the junior high and high school years. It sets their relationship up so Mom remains her daughter's best resource. Camp also focuses on how to talk about and manage three lifelong topics for women: body image, boundaries and boys. The idea behind U & Me Camp is to help our young women have an easier, smoother journey than the women who have gone before them.

I started the session having the girls think of and list all of the characteristics of a best girlfriend: kind, considerate, shares her things, etc. We filled a white board. Then I suggested that the girlfriend change over to a boyfriend. I asked, "What would need to be removed from our white board?" Only one item was suggested to delete! Everyone asks me what the one thing was and I have absolutely no recall. Sorry. (The truth is I was quite surprised about what was unfolding and my mind was spinning.) I then asked, "What, if anything, needs to be added

16

to the list for a boyfriend?" Using a different colored pen, I started adding the ideas the girls threw out. They added at least another 50% of wants and needs to the list. "Can you imagine what a guy would do if he walked in and saw all of these things a girl expects of him?" I asked. We all agreed he would turn around and run out the door!

Later it hit me: *he's not your girlfriend*. Men simply cannot live up to all of the aspects of a relationship that a woman's female friends do, while at the same time deliver an entirely new set on top of that. I had to admit I, too, had carried this fantasy of my husband around for years. I expected him to have all of the traits I loved about my girlfriends *plus* all of the traits I thought were unique to a man. This quite naturally leads us to ask whether there is any overlap between "girlfriend traits" and "boyfriend traits?" Absolutely there is overlap, but it is certainly not the 100% that women too often expect.

What I know now is when I started to consciously acknowledge that there is a difference between my husband and my girlfriends, my relationship experience with my husband changed. I let him off the hook to respond in all the ways I expected my girlfriends to respond. I changed my experience with him forever. You will too.

He Doesn't Know What You Want

There are many reasons that a man doesn't know what the woman he loves wants. And, he doesn't know what she wants in a variety of areas:

- He doesn't know what she wants for her birthday
- He doesn't know what would be the best date of her life
- He doesn't know what household task she wishes he would do

Too often women interpret his not knowing as a sign of the health of the relationship. In other words, she takes it personally. She takes it personally because her girlfriends know what she wants. She takes it personally because she has mentioned her desires to him before, and he still doesn't know what she wants. Her girlfriends always remember. They can even deduce what she would like from a series of clues she has left in numerous conversations.

Typically, his not knowing has nothing to do with how much he likes or cares about a woman. (Unless, of course, "he's just not that into you," and there is an entire book by that title dedicated to that topic.) There are a variety of reasons, all working against him, that keep a man from knowing what his woman wants (like a woman's girlfriend would know). Let's explore them.

He Doesn't Have Relationship Antennas

There's a saying that many people have heard that goes like this:

"If Mama ain't happy, ain't nobody happy!"

While I didn't grow up knowing that, saying it or hearing it around my house, I knew it was true. Girls grow up studying their moms. She is the first woman a girl knows. This is her first occasion at "playing relationship." Mom is complex. There are nuances. Girls know what the tilt of her head, a sigh or a certain tone means. I recall running from my mom when I sensed she was mad, before she had even uttered a word. (This strategy did not help later on with my punishment!) As girls play relationship in their childhood games, they continue to study other girls. Like their moms, girls are also complex and there are lots of nuances. It is as if girls develop huge relationship antennas that are constantly scanning the environment to figure out what would go well, whether it is in a girlfriend relationship, a male-female relationship or her family. It is a critical part of fitting into the girl world for girls to be sensitive towards others and their needs.

Let me give you a few relationship antenna examples. I had a girlfriend who lost her job. I began thinking about what I could do to cheer her up. She is a single gal and I remembered that one time she sent herself flowers for her own birthday. "That's it. I'll send her flowers." I knew flowers would hit the mark because I recalled that she had done that for herself. I have another friend that I bought a birthday card for nine months in advance of her birthday. It was, of course, the perfect card for her. I held it with secret delight for all of those months. I've also been shopping with a friend where she's noticed something that she loves and I told her to get it. When she didn't buy it for herself, I doubled back around in the store and I got it for her. Women admit to me that these are common practices. When I share the birthday card example with audiences, other women in the room begin to nod and laugh. They do it too! These maneuvers represent women playing relationship. Women are subtle in relationships, and they are adept. They also have lots of practice. These examples are not men playing relationship. Boys do not develop these same "relationship antenna" skills as they are playing games of competition. Boys' skills are honed for winning. (I must admit men can and do learn some of these relationship approaches over time. My husband has and it's lovely.) Instead of using antennas, boys learn to experience and practice direct communication.

He Talks Like A Football Huddle

Coupled with the relationship antennas phenomenon, men and women communicate differently. There have been volumes written on gender communication, so I'm not going to go in depth here. I would, though, like to share some stories in a way that might make those communication differences memorable and meaningful. This will help men and women recognize, once again, that he's not your girlfriend.

I did not grow up playing football. However, I think the best way to describe the world of male communication is the football huddle. It seems to me there are some rules about the huddle that are followed, even if they are not written out:

1. In the huddle, one guy at a time speaks. The others listen.
2. The huddle is focused. It is not a consensus situation where various opinions are sought or expressed.
3. The huddle is short. As few words as possible are used to get the point across.
4. The content of what is discussed is factual, not emotional. There is not dialogue about how the others in the huddle feel about what is being said.
5. The huddle does not deal with people dynamics. For example, there is no discussion about if someone was treated unfairly on the last play.

I laugh to myself when I think of how a huddle might go for a group of women:

"How's everyone feeling? That was a hard hit you took. Are you sure you're okay? (Other women would also express their concern for the hit player at this point.) You want to take few plays off? (Other women would offer advice on what might be best for the roughed-up player.) I was thinking we'd do the flea flicker play. What does everyone else think?"

And then the floodgates would open! If you step back and watch a group of men communicate outside of a huddle, you'll hear one man talk at a time. Usually in my live audiences I hear women start laughing at this point. They know when they get in a group, they talk on top of each other and everyone talks at once. The men usually speak one man at a time, and he says a very short sentence. He makes a point. Then the next man speaks about the same topic the previous man has just spoken about. Short, linear, unemotional conversation.

She Talks In Webs And Innuendos

In the female world there is a prevailing style of communication that can be summed us as "Be Nice." At all costs girls want to avoid being labeled "bossy" (or later, "bitchy"). Most girls and women go to the extremes to carry niceness out. Unfortunately there are also girls and women whose natural style does not fit well with this female culture communication style. They have painful experiences with other women, often being told that they run over people, hurt others' feeling or are demanding. In the end, these women report to me that they often feel more comfortable hanging out with men.

Whenever you get women in a group, they are probably talking – many of them – at the same time. The topic goes all over the place. Let's say a group of women are deciding where to go to lunch. "Where should we go?" They all throw out ideas about restaurants, without definitely committing. (That would be "bossy.") Women are very careful not to imply previous suggestions are bad when they bring up their suggestion. (That would be "mean.") And they often bring up ideas about someone else's suggestion. (This is a "play nice" thing to do.) "Oh, that restaurant serves food that is like this place that I went to when I was on vacation." "Where'd you go for vacation?" "I went to Brazil. We had a fabulous time and this happened and that happened." From there someone might point out that a restaurant that was mentioned earlier is by a new store. "What new store?" and then, "I heard they are having a sale."

Are the women ever going to decide on a lunch place? To men listening in, it may seem like they have forgotten the original topic completely. Yes, these women will get to lunch. They will figure that out. It is just women's conversation will have a lot of stops along the way, weaving a web of different conversation threads, whereas men tend to be "bottom line" or direct communicators. The female language style is very much an innuendo, hinting, soft, indirect communication style.

Given all my experience in corporate America, I am a fairly direct, straightforward communicator, yet I catch myself hinting at what I want all of the time. In the midst of a day of projects, when I get hungry for lunch, instead of saying "I'm hungry." I ask others, "Are you hungry? Are you sure you're not hungry?" Or on a road trip when I have to go to the bathroom, I ask, "Does anyone have to go to the bathroom? No, no one needs to go?" My husband drives right by the exit for the bathroom because I haven't said "I have to go to the bathroom." When that happens I realize once again hints don't work effectively with men. Men know that they don't have a clue about what women want. And the truth is it's a woman's role to educate her man quite directly and not with hints.

He's Simple; She's Complex

Beyond communication, men are less complex and more straightforward than women. There is a simple way men communicate this to women, and women don't believe them. When a woman asks a man what he is thinking he may respond, "Nothing." Most women don't believe him! (Male comedians have a field day with this example.) I have posed this scenario to countless men and they admit it is true; they really aren't thinking anything in particular. Men are pretty straightforward with women. We just don't believe them because women are often thinking a million things. (Men also admit to me that they make something up about what they are thinking to satisfy her so she'll stop asking.)

Before this gets misconstrued, I am not saying that men are less smart or any other putdown. When I say, "He's simple," what I mean is he is straightforward and not complex: either black or white, on or off, good or bad. In the male culture men are brought up to express in a narrow emotional range. As Eva pointed out in the Magical Relationship workshop, when women connect with men, they take men on an emotional rollercoaster ride. A woman makes a man's life more fun and more interesting and more of an adventure. Women, too, love adventures and the variety adventures provide. (We will get to more on this in the What About Me & My Needs? chapter in Part III.)

I have a great visual that was used in the Magical Relationships workshop that I love to show in my workshops. I will describe it. Picture a machine that is in the shape of a box. It's about the size of a small microwave. It has two halves. The top half has one switch. The switch is a lever switch that flips up or down to turn it on or off. Up is on; down is off. Can you picture it?

The bottom half of this machine has dials, knobs, buttons, and lights. It has different colors and 20 types of controls that all work differently. The way the machine is labeled is the top half, the one with the single on/off flip switch, is "Man." The bottom half, with all the different colors and varieties of knobs, switches and buttons, is labeled "Woman." I just love this image because I think it really captures visually how we are different.

He Wants To Win (Every Time)

There's good news for women with the male cultural orientation towards winning. An emotionally healthy man translates his desire to win in life into a desire to win with the woman in his life. What does this mean for the woman he's dating or in love with? Glad you asked as it's not what you think and certainly not what is depicted in the mass media. In a relationship, it is the man who typically says,

"I Just Want You To Be Happy"

Just about every woman has heard this or something similar from the man who cares about or loves her. (Remember we're talking about healthy men in relationships. There could be an exception. You may be in a marriage or in a dating relationship with a man who's not emotionally healthy.) There are some other versions of this line:

"Whatever makes you happy" or

"If that will make you happy"

Have you ever heard something like this from the man in your life? Why don't most women believe it when they hear it? (Do you?) As I was facilitating the *Getting The Love You Want and Deserve* relationship series with Linda Binns, we had a brilliant exchange on this idea that I am going to share here. Linda and I had not rehearsed this exchange. She admitted she'd heard the "I just want you to be happy" line from her ex-husband and her current husband. I then surprised her by asking her why she didn't believe it. I wanted to get her candid response. Linda's reaction is so typical of what women in various audiences have shared with me that I'm sharing it verbatim from the transcripts of our workshop.

Linda: "It's not that I don't believe it. I believe that they do want you to be happy. But usually they're saying it when what they're saying or doing beforehand does anything but make you happy. I just don't understand it."

Carolyn: "Okay, so what they're saying or doing doesn't look like the way it should if, in fact, they really do want to make you happy."

Linda: "Right."

Carolyn: "It doesn't maybe look like what you would do if you wanted to make yourself happy, or let's say one of your girlfriends wanted to make you happy—what she would do. Is that true?"

Linda: "That's very true, yes."

Carolyn: "Well it's true for me too. That's why I can throw it out so confidently and know that you would say, 'Well here's why...' Because it's true for most women. [Meaning most women I encounter can justify with examples why they don't believe their man wants to make them happy.] The bottom line here—and I'll just cut to the bottom line, which is a very guy thing to do—is that women and men are different. It's not that men are broken. They're not a broken version of women. And if, as I say that, you find yourself smiling or laughing out loud—when I heard that in the Magical Relationships workshop, I laughed out loud because it was so true for me—if you got an internal smile going inside, a little knowing, a little nodding, or an external, 'Yeah, I always thought they were a little broken.,' then you've got a belief

26

behind this."

Do you genuinely believe your man wants you to be happy?

Winning Means She's Happy

For a man in a relationship, a woman's happiness in her life is a direct measure of whether or not he is winning. When dating, her happiness and *joie de vivre* is also what men are most attracted to in a woman. Contrary to popular belief, it is not the most beautiful woman at the bar that is enticing. The beautiful woman is eye candy only for a time. It is the woman who is having fun, seems happy and is satisfied with herself and her life that most attracts a man. It is the energy that she exudes that is exciting. She is the one he ultimately wants to be with.

Women, and our society as a whole, tease men about wanting to fix things. For a man, the motivation behind fixing things is "I want to fix it for you, so I can win with you, so you'll be happy. When you're happy, I win and I am happy." When I am unhappy in any area of my life, my husband is not winning, even if that area is not directly his responsibility. When I was in a corporate job and I was no longer happy, it had nothing to do with my husband and yet he wanted to fix it. Thus, the best thing we can do as women is to get ourselves to a happy place. Not a fake happy place; I am not talking about making up a happy life or being fake about this. I am talking about being genuinely happy. Possibly some women reading this may be interpreting this as "I'm not supposed to express anything negative in my life." This is not the case. There is a time and a way, though, that will be most effective for him and for you.

Making Him A Winner

The number one way a woman can support her man in feeling like a winner, beyond her own happiness, is with her gratitude for him. This is a man's number one need in a relationship: he wants to be appreciated by the woman in his life. Underneath her gratitude is a tacit sense of approval from the woman that he cares about and loves. My husband, Clint, railed against this idea of needing my approval when he first heard it at Eva & Will's relationship workshop. Yet, as he sat with it, he agreed it is true. Whether men will admit it or not, every man seeks and wants the approval of the woman he is in relationship with. Her appreciation of him, his efforts or anything he is involved with indicates her support and belief in him. This in turn fuels his fire to do more and get more gratitude (and approval).

Why do men need this from their relationships with women? Well Ladies, in case you haven't noticed, it is a tough world for a man. Remember the One-Upmanship Game of having personal comments thrown at you and not taking them personally? Recall that a man monitors what he expresses. He monitors the emotions he shows (as in not crying at all costs) because doing so creates fuel for the future ribbing he may receive. Who, then, are his allies? Where does he get built up in life? His mom, hopefully, and then his girlfriend and then his wife. As we will discuss in various sections of this book, a man will go to great lengths to win, and thus to be appreciated, by his woman. This is good news!

SKILL ALERT: NAG him!

Yes, I want women to NAG men. (Let's reclaim that word for the better, shall we?) I believe there are different levels of winning in a relationship and there are different types of appreciation. Ultimately, this is a skill and it takes practice. Let's explore the dynamics of winning so you can get started with your man. Level 1 Winning has three steps, which I like to remember as "NAG":

1. Notice
2. Acknowledge
3. Gratitude

Step 1: Noticing

The first step appears simple yet may be one of the hardest for most women. She has to *notice* what her man is doing around her and for her and in her life in general. This can be hard, particularly in a relationship that is unbalanced in the workload between them. Many times she is busy doing so many tasks, her man's efforts can seem minimal by comparison. Comparison can also be a slippery slope, because often times when she looks around in a relationship that includes a house, cars, kids and all the upkeep of those things, she is both exhausted and bitter. I admit I often hear a tone creep into a woman's voice when she starts to explain out loud who does what in the household. (Have faith: He Won't Win at House

(Unless You Let Him) is coming in a later chapter.) Interestingly when a woman is dating, she notices every little thing her man does. This is because she is assessing him: Is he for me? Will he make a good life partner/husband/father? For this step I am encouraging a woman to simply notice her man's efforts— without judgment.

Step 2: Acknowledge

After noticing, the next step is to verbally acknowledge to him what she noticed. This is a statement of fact. Since it is true, it should be very easy to report to him. Also, it helps to use a nice tone of voice versus the one with an edge to it. (Ladies, you know what I mean.)

"I see you took out the trash."

"Oh, you emptied the dishwasher."

"You brought the mail in."

One note of caution: it is not a statement of what he also did not do while he was doing what she is acknowledging. I know this from personal experience and years of blowing it. I had a habit of mentioning what Clint did followed by mentioning what else he could have done, or even how he could have done it better.

"Oh, you got the mail and you could have grabbed that flier on the front porch."

"You bathed our daughter and did you change the sheets while she was in the tub?"

"You got the groceries and you didn't grab the laundry at the cleaners next door?"

Do not follow the example lines above. (I put the previous line in italics in case you are scanning this book vs. deep reading it—I don't want any accidental misunderstanding.)

Step 3: Genuinely Appreciate

Admittedly the last step is on par in difficulty with the first step of Noticing. This is where a woman genuinely thanks her man for what he has done. Ladies, be happy, even delighted. Keep the tone of voice upbeat and smile. He will know it is genuine by the *way* she delivers this appreciation as well as the words she uses. Honestly, he will sniff out a faked or inauthentic "thank you." Just because he's not your girlfriend, who has antennas a million miles long for whether someone is being genuine, he is not stupid. He pays attention to voice, body language and then words, so be careful.

Why is a simple "thank you" so hard for some women? What I hear from women, and have experienced in my own life, is when a woman is a living martyr in her relationship, it can be really difficult to thank a man for doing one thing on a list of 100, when she has the other 99 on her list. I am embarrassed to admit that this was true of me. Most women who have some level of success in their work lives find it somewhat difficult to admit that at home she does not have the command she has at the office. Beyond the office, let's face it: most of our mother's were living martyrs. As girls we learned the role and the script. I know I did. When my dad came in the door from work, my mom began pointing out all that was wrong in our family instead of all that was going well. I have a nasty habit of doing the same thing. It's not conscious. The other day I noticed I do it even when my husband calls me in the middle of the day. I'm working to reform this!

I recall thinking that it was impossible and downright stupid to thank my husband for emptying the trash when I had cleaned the house, prepared the meals and done the laundry. My sister summed it up this way, "Appreciating him is just one more thing on my list of things to do!" Her resentment shined through. Can you relate? Initially for me, there was the response in my head and the response that came out of my lips, and they were not the same. Here's what I did to help me bridge the gap. Because I couldn't be genuine about my husband's efforts, I found something I could be genuine about: he was doing it instead of me! This I could be grateful for, and you can too, regardless of how unbalanced things are at home. I recommend that you reflect on the idea that he is doing something—anything—that you are not. Gratitude will bubble up—I encourage you to sit with the idea until it does.

Ladies, this is a new skill and habit, so it will take some time and much attention to establish it. I am here to tell you that you can do it, and the rewards will be worth it. (In case you need immediate reinforcement, please skip to Why Bother? I Can Do It Myself in Part III.)

A Powerful Motivator

Remember the list of 100 things that need doing around the house and in their lives, where he is doing one task and she has the other 99? Imagine this: for the rest of your relationship whatever tasks are on the list, and the way they are currently split between you in your relationship, will remain that way *forever*. Can you live with that? Can you live with that and not turn bitter? Have you noticed this bitterness dynamic in older married couples? I have. (They are my relatives!) When you realize that the only way that anything is going to leave your list and get on your partner's is through meeting his need for appreciation (or by getting an assistant…or as I used to joke, a wife) then it changes the motivation, doesn't it? The truth is you actually know how to NAG already. I mean that in the nicest way, in the new definition of NAG that I have established. When women are with young children who do any project—I don't care what they do or what they make—we find something special about it to point out to them. Why is that? We want to lift them up. We want to make them feel good about their efforts. This gives them confidence to keep going and to do more and risk more.

He's Your Living Gratitude Practice

What if this very thing is what men need too? What if this is what a man needs in the confidence arena with his woman, in his home, in his parenting—in his life? Just because you don't need a thank you for everything you do, doesn't mean he doesn't. (Yes, we will get to your needs in the **What About Me & My Needs?** chapter…or you can jump ahead if you need to.) Just because he isn't your girlfriend does not mean you can skip being nice to him, the way you are nice to your girlfriends. When you know something is important to your girlfriend, you say it to her, give it to her, do it for her, etc. Remember when I said that a man's desire to win is good news for women? Well, there's also bad news for women: this need to win for men is "insatiable." This is the exact word Eva used in her workshop around men needing appreciation. Over time I have decided it best applies to the entire gamut of winning. Dictionary.com defines insatiable in this way:

in·sa·tia·ble [in-**sey**-shuh-buh l, -shee-uh-]

adjective not satiable; incapable of being satisfied or appeased: *insatiable hunger for knowledge.*

Or in this case one might say, "A man has an insatiable hunger for winning and he most wants to with his woman." This word still haunts me. That is why I am sharing it with you. For perfectionists (like me) out there, please know that he won't ever win with you every time. You are, alas, both human. Please don't set that standard for yourself. (Might I point out that most sports teams don't win every time? Even if they do in one season, they rarely repeat it in the next.) The bottom line is you could not *ever* demonstrate enough—with your gratitude or praise—that he's winning (in your whole lifetime). You may remember that Oprah started a gratitude practice for millions of women. It turns out he's your living gratitude practice.

He Needs A Radar Reading

A man really wants to be a woman's hero. He wants to be loved. He wants a smiling woman who adores him. He needs a woman to focus on what she wants, not on what she doesn't want. Fortunately, there is a tool to get women there. Remember men want to win, and they are pretty gun-shy when it comes to women and relationships. They might come off as confident and joking; however, especially on the romantic side they're often reluctant about what to do. If a woman can point him in the right direction to meet her needs, then he knows "No matter what, I'm going to win." Often times a woman doesn't give a man the help he needs because she is testing whether or not he is broken. (More on that coming in the *He's Not Broken* chapter in Part III.)

SKILL ALERT: Radar Reading

What men need from women is a Radar Reading. Initially this tool is a favorite of men's and once women experience its results, it is a favorite of women's too. I'm not going to lie. It takes women a bit of practice to feel comfortable using this tool because it can seem bossy or demanding—two things women never want to be accused of. I consider a Radar Reading Level II Winning. It is giving your man proactive ways to win with you in a variety of arenas. Before I explain the skill and how to do it, let me offer a few words of caution. *Do not* begin using

Radar Readings on your man until you have practiced NAGing
him. Yes, the new form of NAGing: Notice, Acknowledge &
Gratitude. (Bet you never thought you'd be encouraged to
practice NAGing!) He needs experience winning with you
consistently. He also needs to gain confidence knowing he is
safe enough to take a risk with you. In this case, "safe" means
that he wins when he risks—make no mistake about it.
Reversing the order of Level I (NAG) and Level II (Radar
Reading) Winning does not work, even for Type A over
achievers. It doesn't matter if you feel more interested in Radar
Readings and more capable of pulling them off. (If you are still
skeptical, please skip ahead to the chapter titled *"He's Not Doing
What I Asked!"* and read all of the reasons why running before you
walk with your man, so to speak, will not put you ahead.)

Step One: Scan Yourself

Think of a Radar Reading like the radar that is used at
airports. Airport radar scans the sky and gives an image of
everything that is on the horizon. It also shows the location of
one object relative to another. A radar reading is something a
woman does to scan herself and her life. (If you are a male
reader, you can teach a woman to do this for you.) She is
looking for what is on her horizon that would bring her joy,
that would bring her happiness. It could be experiences she
wants to have, like going on a hike or to an event or movie. It
could be material items she'd like to own, such as new piece of
artwork or a smoothie blender or a new cell phone. It could be
clothing or shoes or jewelry. It could be a project that she
would like done around the house, such as having a room

painted a different color or planting a rose bush. It really doesn't matter what she comes up with. Her ideas will likely be a combination of small delights and big items or projects. Her Radar Reading will be entirely unique to her. The point is that she needs to determine what would enhance her life right now. To be honest, when Eva introduced the idea of asking for what I want, using various tools and approaches, I was a little intimidated. I felt asking directly would be really demanding on Clint. It wasn't until I had been practicing giving Clint wins, NAGing him, for about a month that I decided to give Radar Readings a try. To be completely honest, it was also because we had an anniversary coming up.

Female readers, take a moment to attempt this. Scan your life and come up with 3-5 things that would delight you. If you have paper and a pen, write them down. By the way, Radar Readings can get outdated; what is on her radar now may not be there in six months. In my experience, many men already understand that the woman he is with is a moving target; it is the woman who does not realize this about herself.

Step 2: Share Your Radar Reading

Now that you have some ideas about what would delight you, the next step is to share what you have discovered with your man. Radar Readings are only valuable if they are shared. Otherwise, a woman can feel frustrated discovering all of the things she would like to have in her life and recognizing she doesn't have them. Worse still, she may decide to take matters into her own hands and get them for herself. This is a mistake I made and I will share more about later.

There are unlimited ways to share a Radar Reading with a man. Good news Ladies: you can share your Radar Readings in whatever way you choose. No matter the approach, the excitement and energy that you show him about your Radar Reading will motivate him, reminding him that these are ways he can win with you. He watches the expression on your face and pays attention to your tone of voice, so allow your excitement to come through in as many ways as possible. I like to think about a little girl asking her daddy for ice cream. She bubbles over, jumping up and down showing her excitement about her idea. At some point all women used to be that little girl, so I know you know how to express excitement and enthusiasm. If you have forgotten, watch little girls as they ask for something. They are quite good teachers in this arena. I am not suggesting a woman jump up and down like a little girl, unless that continues to be a natural style of hers. What I am suggesting is that she doesn't quell her excitement, as I used to do. I noticed that the more important something was to me, the more serious, and stoic, I would get when bringing it up with Clint. It was as if I were behaving the same way I would when presenting a business proposal to a management team—not motivating!

I want to give some ideas, and later some of my own examples, for how a woman can deliver a Radar Reading. Luckily for me a Radar Readings doesn't have to be delivered in person, because I was initially not ready for that. I have learned that when I share them in person, my husband pays attention to *how* I deliver my ideas. If I read him my ideas, he pays attention to my facial expression and voice inflections. Later he tells me, "I did that idea first because I noticed you were really excited when you said that." I might not have realized I treated any item in my Radar Reading differently than another. A man looks for any and all clues from his woman because he wants to win. As an aside, when I read a Radar Reading, Clint always asks me for whatever I've written it on, so I have learned to put it on fun paper or write with different colored markers—anything to put some good energy into it for him as he's contemplating it and perhaps doubting whether he can deliver.

You can write your Radar Reading down for him. You can send him on a treasure hunt to discover your ideas one at a time. You can deliver them via U.S. mail, email, drawings, a series of text messages or a picture board. You can read your ideas to him. However, as you share them, it is important that you put some excited energy into your Radar Reading. Your excited energy is his motivation; it fuels him and his desire to win with you. It also changes the feel of a Radar Reading from a demand list to an enticing shared adventure that leads to a win for him and a win for you. You are allowing him to deliver more of what you want in your life. It's a win-win.

For me, figuring out how to share a Radar Reading is the best part. I have a few examples coming up that should help get some of your own creative juices flowing. The important point is that you are letting your man know what would be fun and interesting for you. When I am doing this for my husband, I am proactively giving him ways to win with me. Because I am not artistically inclined *at all,* I typically use only words and attempt to put them on nice paper or deliver them in a unique way. That is my way. Other women are really "artsy and craftsy" and have done amazing things with their Radar Readings. One of my clients who loves to play games created a date night game board with a spinner where any idea the spinner landed on would be a fun date idea for her.

Whatever your style, here are some tips for sharing Radar Readings in a way that helps motivate your man to win with you:

- ◆ Keep it light
- ◆ Have fun with it
- ◆ Be creative in your approach
- ◆ Let your excitement and energy shine through

Step 3: Reward Movement

The final step is to reward any action your man takes towards an item on your Radar Reading with enthusiastic support of him and confidence in his ability to deliver it to you. Because of the One-Upmanship game, boys become quite adept at posing as confident and secure. This quite naturally carries over into all the areas of their lives. The truth is, our men are romantically gun-shy and often doubt themselves. Remember, he didn't grow up playing relationship. When he is first presented with the ideas in your Radar Reading, he may be like one of the old vehicles that had a manual choke. Am I dating myself with this example? In case I am, we had an old Toyota Land Cruiser that had a choke knob we pulled, then I pumped and pumped the gas while turning the key over and over again, while the engine sputtered until it finally roared to life. Your man may "sputter" before he kicks into gear. At this point, ignore whatever he says. His initial reluctance is his doubt. Continue with your faith in his ability to pull off whatever your heart's desire is. This was initially very hard for me to do. When given a request, I remembered my dad "sputtered" a lot. After years of listening to my mom and him, he drove me crazy, because I interpreted it as complaining or not wanting to do what he was asked. When I got married and Clint sputtered about anything, I interpreted it the same way. I was determined to not repeat in my marriage what I had grown up around, so I came up with what I thought was a great solution—I simply did whatever the task was myself. There are so many problems with that solution, the biggest of which is that over time my list got so long that I became resentful. The other, as you hopefully already thought of, is I stole from Clint many of the ways he could win with me. Eventually I learned that sputtering is part of Clint's, my dad's and all men's process. Instead of thinking of it as complaining, I have learned to interpret it as a cry for encouragement. Clint needs me to demonstrate faith in him until he gains confidence in himself. This is something he will never ask me for directly. Fortunately, using my highly tuned relationship antennas, I can recognize when my support is needed and give it to him. You can too. Many of my female clients have an Aha! moment of compassion when they learn to translate sputtering into what it truly is—a cry for support. For my mom this understanding has come too late; she is still annoyed when she hears my dad sputtering and is tempted to take on the project or task herself. Using different approaches and responses are skills, I remind her, and building skills takes time and patience.

After you have delivered your Radar Reading, your man needs encouragement from you. He needs appreciation. He needs your continued excitement about the end goal. For me, this was no small task. Beyond my gut reaction to Clint's sputtering, I already mentioned I would ask in a subdued, almost business-like manner and then get really quiet about what I had asked for. In truth, I think it was because I was afraid if I brought my idea up again, Clint might change his mind or get upset, as I had witnessed my dad doing. (There is more coming on the impact our family experiences have on our current relationship in the Culture Matters section.) I attribute another pitfall for me to being a strong-willed, capable woman. Once I discovered what I wanted by doing a scan of my life, I wanted it immediately. I was used to getting things for myself on my own time schedule. Like other women of my generation, I worked and had the financial means to buy things. I also had a variety of handyman skills, thanks to my parents for involving me in doing all sorts of tasks around their rental properties and our house. When Clint didn't act fast enough on something, I had formed the habit of assuming he wasn't going to handle it, and I did it myself. There was lots of "me, myself and I" going on in my marriage and this is not how I ultimately wanted to live.

What I have learned is that after delivering a Radar Reading, the following list helps remind me to support Clint and curb myself from stepping in:

- ◆ NAG (Notice, Acknowledge, Gratitude) him for any and all actions he takes towards what you want
- ◆ Be flexible with regards to the timing he delivers on
- ◆ Allow him room to do it his way (which likely won't be the way you might have done it for yourself)

We will be exploring the last two points in depth in Part II: Living Our Differences.

The Pressure's On

Women need to do Radar Readings proactively. Any time a man needs to give a woman a present, or any of the occasions where there is some sort of romantic expectation, is a time when she can help set her man up to win. There are four occasions where she must give her man help in winning with her. She must help him because the pressure is on for him to deliver big results to her. Either she is putting the pressure on him by her heightened expectations or society is or, worst of all, both. These occasions are:

1. Her birthday
2. The holidays (Christmas, Hanukah, Easter, Mother's Day)
3. Valentine's Day
4. Their anniversary

Post-It Notes & Lipstick Story

I mentioned earlier that I first attempted a Radar Reading because our anniversary was coming. I wanted to be creative. I knew that the more energy and excitement I put into the asking, the more motivated Clint would be. I was also concerned that I could not deliver a Radar Reading in person without it sounding like a demand notice, so I knew I wasn't ready for an in-person delivery. Instead I got some pink Post-It Notes that were in the shape of lips. I put one idea on each Post-It Note. Then I put some bright red lipstick on. I decided to go all out. With my bright red lipstick on, I kissed all the places where I knew he would go throughout his morning routine. I put the lip-shaped Post-It Notes everywhere along his path too. I gave him a bunch of ideas, big and small. My thinking was that he would pick a couple of ideas, confident that he could win with me. I thought about what would feel romantic to me and included anything that would have delighted me. In many cases I kept the categories really broad: romantic music, flowers, champagne. In the end, he delivered every single thing on those Post-It Notes. This was not my intention and that is not the point I want to make. I am sharing my results to let you know how motivated he was. He was so excited because I don't think my husband had won very much with me in our relationship, so it was motivational for him that he could do these things and be assured of the win.

In addition to a Post-It Note with the word "flowers," one of the other items on a note was "Calla Lilies" because they were the flowers we had at our wedding. At noon the day of my anniversary the doorbell rang and it was the flower delivery man. I had gotten some Calla Lilies. I assumed this was my entire gift and I was thrilled. I called him "Oh my gosh! These are great. They are gorgeous. How romantic!" It was not hard for me to be genuinely grateful and enthusiastic because I had not received Calla Lilies from him since our wedding. When he came home later that day, he brought me not one, not two, but three different silk flower arrangements. One of them had silk Calla Lilies because, he explained to me, my fresh Calla Lilies were going to die. One of the arrangements was a pot of daisies because he knows daisies are my happy flower. The third set was a bunch of yellow flowers so I could have cheery flowers in my home office on the days I worked from home. I was floored by this man who, once given a direction, had really run with it. I was in tears by the time we got in the car to go on our anniversary date. He turned on the stereo and "our song," the one we danced to at our wedding 15 years earlier, was playing. It was an old Aretha Franklin song and not one we owned in our music collection. I had no idea how he hunted it down, as it was long past being popular and iTunes wasn't invented yet. One of the items on my Post-It Notes had been romantic music and he hit the bull's eye. On our date he had a bottle of Veuve Clicquot, which is my favorite champagne, brought to the table. And—I just love this!—he had an extra bottle to share over weekend, because our anniversary falls over a three-day holiday weekend. All of this from a Post-It Note that read "champagne." I could go on and on about this one experience. The bottom line is I was convinced. I saw what could happen when I provided some direction and got out of the way to let my husband deliver and win with me.

Hershey's To The Rescue Story

Another Radar Reading I delivered was lots of fun for both of us. There was no special occasion for the reading other than to give him some ideas for how to win with me. It is important that a man wins on a day-in, day-out basis versus only on special occasions. If you like to have fun—who doesn't? — consider this. My husband loves sweets, so I bought a bag of mini Hershey's chocolate bars. I unwrapped each one and on the inside of the wrapper wrote a different idea I had about what would be fun in my life and bring me joy. By the way, I was not used to thinking about what I wanted in my life. I have found this is true of many women. At first it took me some time to come up with more than a couple of ideas. The only reason I kept attempting to add more ideas is that I wanted Clint to have a range of ways to delight me. Otherwise, he would have a very narrow set of ideas and, once again, I feared it would feel like a demand list. I put all of the chocolates in a cookie jar that sits in his office. One of the ideas was a spontaneous lunch date. One day, in the middle of the day, I was working from home and he showed up. I was so excited. "Oh my gosh you're here for our spontaneous lunch date!" He could tell I was genuinely excited because we had always planned our work-week activities, so this spontaneous approach was special for me. I love surprises and it felt like a surprise. He rolled right into the spontaneous lunch date. Weeks later I learned that he had not opened that chocolate yet, so he did not know that one of my ideas was a spontaneous lunch date. He had merely stopped by to say hello on his way across town. However, I was so happy about the idea of lunch together that he took me out to lunch. I thanked him so much about lunch that when he went back to his office where the cookie jar was, he unwrapped the rest of the chocolates so he had all of the ideas. Talk about a motivated man! I had figured out a way to make the Radar Reading fun for me to share and also fun for him to receive. Again and again I have been delighted by what Clint has done that goes beyond my ideas I have shared in the Radar Readings.

Now my husband shares with other guys, "It's the best thing to get a Radar Reading. You always know that you're going to win. You always know that you are going to be a hero with her, that she's going to be happy." Beyond Radar Readings for pressure-filled occasions, some other areas where a woman might consider giving her man ways to win with her are: around the house, date ideas, child rearing and vacations.

Living The Endless Date Tips

Mastering any skill is usually easier when you have some tips for doing well. At one of my Women's Aha! retreats I taught a class called *Living The Endless Date*. As part of the class I taught women to deliver a Radar Reading for dates. They did it using a poster board cut in half and drawing ideas or cutting out pictures that represented things that they would love to do for dates. Clint and I were about to go on a trip to San Diego, so I created a Radar Reading about all of the things I wanted to experience in San Diego: a walk along the beach, a meal at an authentic Mexican restaurant, a shared sunset, shopping, etc. This way he could win with me on vacation, and I could win too. As I was creating my picture board, I realized how many expectations I had around our vacation together, and I hadn't shared any of them. I expected Clint to know exactly what to do with me to make a beach vacation wonderful. (I know—he's not my girlfriend!) During the class some of the women suggested they really weren't creative and doubted whether they could deliver Radar Readings in all of the different ways I had mentioned. Radar Readings are not a contest and no one is being graded. Once they got started with the colored markers and the magazine pictures, they realized that there are no hard and fast rules for sharing them—anything that would make their hearts sing qualified. That's true for you too. Give yourself a break about how you share your ideas and start, as I did, with something that will be fun and easy for you.

I am just about to deliver to my husband a Radar Reading on dates. I've decided that I want to go on some different dates, as we can get into a rut and do the dinner-out date endlessly. If I say to Clint, "Honey, you need to take me on some different dates" boy does that put the pressure on! He could win. He may not win. A different way of saying is, "Honey, I've been thinking about going on some dates." When I say that, there's a smile on my face and playfulness in my voice. There's some excitement because I am excited about the idea of new date experiences, so I let that excitement shine through when I talk about them. Next I am going to share with him some of my ideas. I'm not sharing down to the tiniest detail because then it feels more like a test: "Can you jump through all of the hoops exactly as I've laid them out and do the exact date that I want?" No. That is not getting out of the way and allowing him to deliver. That is testing him. That is a woman testing her man to see if he really loves her. It also means that he actually hasn't taken "date planning" off of her list of things to do. She is still doing all of the thinking and simply getting him to execute. Women often report to me that simply having their man execute would be a vast improvement over how things are currently done in their relationship. If you can relate, I promise you that is aiming too low. I know because I did that—for years!

I'm going to say, "You know, Honey, I love going out on the boat for a date." That's all I will say. I will point him in the direction of the boat for a great date. Whatever he shows up with—if he arranges for music, brings some flowers, a picnic dinner, something to drink—I have left open for him. I just gave him a clue "Let's go on a boat date." Some of you are skeptical thinking, "Well my husband would just show up with the boat and that would be our date. He wouldn't have thought through the other things." Maybe, maybe not. My experience is that when I give my husband a clue *and he knows he's going to win*, he goes for the over-delivery. As the woman I am going to give him a win no matter what. Let's say on the first boat date he shows up with a bottle of champagne. I'm going to say, "Oh my gosh—you thought of a bottle of champagne? That is so much fun. Thank you. I love that!" He is going to win with me big on the champagne because you know what? Next time he is going to show up with champagne and something else. Test it for yourself and see.

Men want to delight their women and they do not necessarily know how. Once pointed in the right direction, they can take it from there. It is that simple. Men are simple. The happier that she can be and allow herself to be, and the more she can allow him to deliver for her, the better relationship they will have. The more motivated he is going to be to do it over and over and over again. I'm telling you, it works. And the results in your life are worth a few extra pleases and thank you's.

Part II

Living Our Differences

He Loves To Deliver (When He Wins)

Coupled with this idea of winning, men are compulsive about getting things done. At this point women usually say, "Are you kidding? I have a list of 25 things. What do you mean they're compulsive about getting things done? I've wanted him to do this one thing forever and he hasn't gotten it done." I had that same reaction when Eva and Will brought this up in their workshop. What I want to point out is that men like to have a mission that they *complete*. They are not like women. They do not have 10 missions going on at once. They have one mission that they like to finish before beginning the next one. For example, a mission is a project he is working on at home, like replacing the plumbing inside of a toilet or cleaning the garage. (Cliché enough for you?) Men are compulsive about completing missions. They wait to complete one mission before moving on to the next. Men are often teased about their inability to multitask. Women even complain about it as if, once again, men are broken and they need fixing: "If he could just learn to multitask!" You know what? He will not. Most men will not learn to multitask. If women would just let that go, we can be a lot happier because men are not broken. They are not our multitasking girlfriends. They are different.

Research has shown us that men's brains work differently than women's. There is starting to be more and more research on that and more books on it too. One of the early books that I appreciated on this topic is called *The Female Brain* by Louanne Brizendine (Morgan Road Books, 2006). Without going into the brain science of it all, the connections in our brains are different. What anyone can notice without ever reading a medical journal or a book on this topic is that men are focused. Once they engage in a mission, they do not like to break away from their missions until they are finished. Focus is really a tremendous gift that men have and can bring—if it is honored.

Do Not Interrupt A Man On A Mission

Men get pretty frustrated when they are doing a mission and it gets interrupted. If you are going to interrupt him in the midst of something, he is not going to get what he wants and you are not either. This was a big eye-opener in our lives. Shortly after this understanding came via the Magical Relationships class, Clint and I were redoing some steps on our back patio. What you need to know for this story to have meaning is Clint is a man who eats his meals by the clock. It doesn't matter if we slept-in and had breakfast at 10:00; at noon it is time for lunch. While we were doing our back step project, I noticed it was 2 o'clock, and I realized that I was hungry. Because I communicate like a woman—recall the **He Doesn't Know What You Want** chapter— instead of saying, "I'm hungry, Honey." I said, "Are you hungry?" (Uug!) Quite honestly I *knew* he'd be hungry because we were already past his standard lunch time. To my shock, he declined lunch. Not one to give up, I kept pushing him, "Are you sure you're not hungry?" Then it hit me. He was in the middle of delivering on the mission of our back steps and he did not want to be interrupted—even for food! This was such a great example for

54

me because he is typically quite sensitive to the time he eats. It was the first time that I understood the power of a man being engaged in something.

Another dynamic to understand is that men go from one mission to the next in a serial fashion. Have you ever stopped to notice that about a man? He does yard work. He cleans the ducts. He starts dinner. This is not at all how I do projects throughout a day. In fact, it can look like a tornado blew through the house if someone stops by at the wrong moment. I turn on the washer and then head into the bedroom to grab the pile of laundry that needs sorting. In the midst of this, I recall I need to throw something in the crock pot for dinner if it's going to be done in time. While doing that I notice that the screw is loose on a cabinet handle, so I traipse out to the garage for a tool. While in the garage I notice that I forgot to unpack the crate from my workshop the night before, so I begin that task. In the end, all of the projects get done, most likely not in the order they were started. I admit, too, that sometimes I forget one of my projects and remember I was in the midst of it only when I come upon it later. (Too often this happens when I lift the lid of the washer and discover the cycle has run with no clothes in it!) Men watch women do this whirlwind of projects and shake their heads in wonder.

What I do for Clint and other men in my life, whether friends or business colleagues, is stop to acknowledge what they are working on and ask if I can interrupt. I even do this with my dad when I call him on the phone. "Have I caught you at an okay time? Can I catch you for a few minutes?" The old me would have launched into a conversation without so much as a thought about what my dad was doing in his office on the other end of the phone. It is quite simply a matter of asking if he is at a point for being interrupted or not. A man can interrupt his mission. Sometimes, though, it is really hard for him to stop. Other times it is fine. This is an area, by the way, that I can be male-like in my concentration. Typically if I am doing a large work project that has an approaching deadline, it is best not to interrupt me. (Clearly, given my earlier example, it is not when I do the laundry!)

He's A Delivery Man

To take this a little bit further, when men are doing these missions they are doing what I refer to as "delivering in life." Men love to deliver. They were born to deliver, meaning to accomplish something. They accomplish little missions all the time. When they are doing that, when they are delivering on a mission, they are winning. Thus when a woman acknowledges her man as he completes his mission, he has gotten her gratitude, and thus her approval. The best part is he will repeat the cycle over and over and over again—because men are insatiable about winning and because it feels good to be appreciated. The other thing that I want to acknowledge is that in order for a man to deliver, a woman has to give him room to deliver. I think this is another area that becomes a test for strong, capable women. I know that was the case for me. As I have shared earlier, I often did not give Clint room to deliver for me and thus to get my acknowledgement and gratitude. I am a very capable woman. Beyond doing projects for my parents, this may have come from years of wanting to prove to my older brothers, and even our chauvinistic foreign exchange student, that I could do anything they could do. Over the years

I have learned to do just about anything, including plumbing and wiring. When your man is doing a project for you, it does not matter whether or not you can also do it or even if you can do it better. Your focus needs to change. You are not, after all, competing with him, as I was with my brothers. You are in relationship with him.

I'm Right; You're Wrong

As an example, when I asked my husband, Clint, to do a project, I had in my mind how it would go. I pictured a single trip to Home Depot to get whatever parts we needed and then he could complete the project. The reality is Clint went to Home Depot five different times. I got frustrated and let him know he didn't have to do it like that. Without understanding it, I was critiquing his mission as he went along. At that time it did not matter if I actually got *what* I had asked for because I did not like *how* it was done. Do you ever find you are as caught up in the way something is done versus achieving the end goal itself? (The He Won't Win At House (Unless You Let Him) chapter addresses this pitfall.) I felt my way was more efficient, and I pointed that out. As you may have guessed, while I was pointing out more efficient ways, Clint was not winning with me. He was not winning during the entire project. Even if I were to compliment him and show my gratitude for him at the end of the project, it did not feel good to him. I, on the other hand, was determined to point out to Clint how right I was. When a woman is holding the idea of "I'm right; you're wrong" there is never room for her man to get a win.

Retiring The Improvement Queen

When a woman gives a man something to do, she needs to get out of the way and let him handle it. As I emphasized in the Radar Readings examples, any movement towards accomplishing what she has asked for—any movement—that is met with compliments and gratitude will motivate him to keep going. The minute the criticism starts, she is likely to have him stop the project or at the very least she will experience a huge shift in his attitude towards the project. Even a simple suggestion of "Or you could do it this way" may shut him down. I know this first hand. I can be "The Improvement Queen" with my helpful hints and suggestions. After showering them on Clint, his entire demeanor would change. My girlfriends always welcomed my suggestions. I didn't understand what was wrong with him (because of course I had given him great ideas). I didn't recognize that for Clint, my suggestions were experienced as criticism. That is why his attitude changed. The more I suggested, the more he shut down until finally he would give me his fallback line, "Whatever you want." While this line may sound lovely as you read it in this book, the tone of his delivery was not: short, terse and frustrated. (This line is actually equivalent to, "I'm done trying to win with you," though he doesn't say it out loud.) I had a visceral reaction because that response implied that I was being bossy and demanding—maybe even bitchy? That's what my relationship antennas suggested to me. We've already covered girls and women want to avoid appearing those ways at all costs, even if they're not openly accused of that behavior. At this point, I joined Clint in frustration. Here I was being a helpful wife, and I felt I was being criticized and rejected. This would have been a great time to exercise The Benefit Of The Doubt Rule that you will read about in the chapter He Won't Win At House (Unless You Let Him). I'll admit that for endless cycles of these types of exchanges, neither of us extended the benefit of the doubt, and neither of us was winning, especially he with me. Instead we offered each other a frosty politeness through the end of the projects, while each of us seethed underneath.

Not offering unsolicited ideas while Clint is in the middle of delivering a mission has been one of the biggest adjustments for me. Anyone who knows me knows I love ideas and I have a million of them for nearly every occasion. My phone calls with close girlfriends always include a rundown of my latest discoveries. My mom is an accomplice in ideas exploration with me. She loves clever ideas and forwards emails or sends envelopes of clippings with new, unique approaches to everything from cleaning the house to raising our daughter to investing strategies—she has ideas for everything! Women also quite naturally openly share all sorts of tips with each other when raising children. They exchange best approaches for diaper rash, pacifier eradication, potty training, temper tantrums, sibling rivalry—the list is endless.

Men do not give each other unsolicited advice. I recently pointed this out to my mom when she suggested Clint call my dad to help him with a legal matter. Mom reasoned that since Clint's an attorney, he may have a different perspective to share that would be valuable to Dad. The truth is that Clint probably does have a useful viewpoint. In that moment, though, I could hear Clint's likely response, "I'm not going to call him. Your dad can call me if he wants my advice." This isn't withholding in the male culture. This is courtesy. This is an honoring signal that the other man is capable of handling his own problems.

When Clint is involved in a project, I attempt to remember how suggestions work for him. Don't get me wrong; a woman can offer advice and ideas to her man. Unsolicited advice, though, may be misinterpreted as criticism, particularly if it comes in a torrent, as mine often does. Idea after idea rolls off my tongue. What works best is when I ask before the mission begins, "What are you thinking about how this project is going to go?" We then happily engage in a back-and-forth exchange of ideas. To be assured of success during a mission, I do best when I ask permission to share my ideas, "Love, can I share some ideas I have about this?" I admit it still kills me when he doesn't take me up on hearing my ideas. I'm working on this reaction! To get past feeling excluded when he's not open to my ideas, I remind myself: 1) I don't want this entire job; 2) Clint over-delivers when I get out of his way; 3) We are both happier when I retire as The Improvement Queen.

Complimenting and acknowledging him is important not only at the end of the project or a mission; it is important that gratitude and support comes from his woman throughout his mission. At this point you may be thinking, as I did, all of this acknowledging and complimenting and leaving him alone to do it his way on his schedule is too much. You could do the project more easily and efficiently yourself. Hold tight. As enticing as you doing it yourself might sound, the chapter called He's A Lot Of Overhead is dedicated to illustrating why this might not be your best option.

Ladies, it is your job to assign the missions via Radar Readings and reward his progress and completion with a win. Anything else is stealing from his sense of delivering and winning with you as well as stealing from your long-term happiness—and his.

He Puts His Attention Where He Is Winning

One day in the midst of an intense work day, I learned one of my female colleagues, Karen, was getting a divorce. I heard, and later she confirmed, that they were not having marital problems nor were either of them involved in an affair. He walked in one night, told her he was "done" and their marriage ended. Just like that. Karen's story haunted me. What if Clint walked in one day and announced he was "done?" No counseling. No second chances. Done. Over. Gone.

Admittedly this ending bothered me because I was often working long hours (like Karen did), arriving home after Clint, working late into the night as he slept as well as getting up before the alarm went off to complete work assignments. What if Clint was growing tired of my schedule without my knowing it? What if he was close to "done" and wasn't admitting it? What if Clint's being "done" came upon him suddenly, with no warning for him either? These fears haunted me. If I weren't so busy at work, I am sure I would have become hysterical about them. What this story did was rock my security; a key need of women's that I touch on in the Keep Me Safe section. The idea of Clint suddenly leaving also triggered my amygdala, the portion of the brain associated with storing information to help keep a person safe, among other things. Needless to say, Karen's story remained in the back of my thoughts long after her divorce was finalized. This is why when Eva and Will explained that men put their attention where they are winning, I perked up and paid close attention.

   We have already covered at great length a boy's desire to win and how important winning is to men. Its makes perfect sense to me that a man will continue wanting to win, even if he is no longer winning with the woman in his life. In my own family I saw my brothers switch from playing one sport to another when their skills in a sport were not strong enough to keep pace with the other boys' talents. Indeed, in our house we had a Peanuts poster of Snoopy walking off of the tennis court with a caption that read, "Show me a good loser and I'll show you a real loser." Need I say more?

   I began to reframe my childhood. My dad was greeted at the door each night by a wife sharing what was going wrong around the house. When we sat down to the dinner table the dynamics of a blended family began, as tension ran high between my mom and my stepbrother. Believe me when I say my mom was not happy. Every night my dad went back to work. I thought every dad did that until I broadened my horizons as I grew older. Later I simply thought Dad was a workaholic. Perhaps he was. I also knew, though, that he won at work. That may have fed his ability to work long hours. He was a senior partner. He was selected to sit on a national executive board for his firm. He was respected in the business community and the treasurer for every business organization he belonged to. I can see now how winning at work and in the community was more attractive.

   Other men turn to different activities besides work to keep winning when they are not winning at home. Some become avid golfers. Where I live in the United States, men can fish and hunt incessantly. I have had women ask if a deep interest in an activity means that he is putting his attention elsewhere because he is not winning with her. My answer is that only she will know that. Only she will know if he is winning at home with her, if he is still motivated to meet her needs and get a win. Clint loves to fish and hunt. He loves golf. He is also incredibly respected in his career. He engages his other pursuits, though, in moderation. He balances his time doing his work activities and personal interests with his family time. Because of Karen's sudden marriage ending—and who knows what the entire story of that truly was—I have always been clear that I want Clint's attention to go to me first and foremost. If he ever drifts, even a little, I check in with myself on how things are going with me on the winning front. Am I doing my part to notice, acknowledge and be grateful, to NAG him? Am I delivering Radar Readings that help him stay engaged and on track to win with me?

I have always been clear that I am not interested in the worst case scenario: Clint puts his attention with another woman whom he wins with. I have often heard women criticize a man who has had an affair and then after the divorce continues his relationship with the other woman. Often they will point out how good he had it before with his wife who did everything for him. Now, they point out, he is constantly jumping through hoops and doing things to please this new woman. I see it differently. I wonder if he feels needed and he is winning with the new woman. Please understand me. I am not condoning extramarital affairs. I am not blaming women for the break up of their marriages. While I have not personally experienced a divorce, I grew up split between blended families, so I know there are many dynamics at play in divorces. What I like to remember to help keep my own marriage on track is that for a man winning is insatiable.

He Won't Lead At Intimacy

In the book *Outliers* (Little, Brown & Company, 2008) author Malcolm Gladwell points out there is more to success than meets the eye or what the newscasters portray. One concept from this book that has caught on and even become a popular catch phrase is "10,000 hours." Gladwell explains that across professions, sports and music, studies have shown that to gain mastery and become a world-class expert in virtually any arena, one must dedicate 10,000 hours of practice and hard work.

10,000 Hours

When it comes to intimacy in relationships, women have 10,000 hours in by the time they finish 6th grade! Men don't. Boys don't typically play intimacy when they are playing competition. Beyond their relationship with their parents, or perhaps a trusted relative (aunt, sister, grandma), the first intimacy a man has is when dating begins. Let's look at this. When boys are in the football huddle, they are not checking in on emotions: "How are you feeling about the way he is blocking you?" or "Are you okay or do you need some time to ground yourself?" Never happened! (Huge violation of football huddle rules.) Yet we expect men to take the lead in relationships, as in lead the way.

Conversely for girls, and later women, the path of intimacy

is quite natural. She's experienced intimacy before hundreds of times while hanging out with girlfriends or at a sleepover party, swapping stories of her dreams, her crushes, her disappointments—her life. Is that what he's done while hanging out with his friends? No way. (We covered this in **He Didn't Play With Dolls**, so if you need a refresher, reread that chapter.)

Am I giving women one more thing to own here: intimacy? Nope. What I am pointing out is that her experience level with this topic is vastly different than his. Women rarely—ever?—stop to take this into account. Neither do men. Let's explore it together. We've already established that a healthy man's deepest pleasure and desire is to win with the woman in his life—every time, all the time. And remember a very important point is he will put his attention where he is winning, so she wants to make sure it is with her. We've also covered that he doesn't necessarily know how to win with her, unless she tells him. Further, sometimes it is hard for a woman to know what she wants and then to articulate it to her man. It is hard to be clear about what she wants and often times easier to communicate what she *does not* want. Even when a woman has been clear and he knows what she wants, he then faces his next hurdle: can I deliver it to her? And, we have already covered that it is not part of the male culture to openly share performance doubts.

Not Bought At The Store

Intimacy is built as a collection of shared moments and experiences. It builds over time and there is no formula. Simply put, intimacy is the glue of a relationship that cannot be bought at the store. It is not something that is made at a garage workbench either. Worse still, more than likely he has no experience from his boyhood friendships at building intimacy without the aid of some sort of team experience, athletic or scholastic, or fraternal membership. While he may have enjoyed the results of the intimacy that existed, he likely was not actively thinking of or paying attention to how much intimacy existed or how it was created. Contrast that with girls, who often leave friendships behind if there is not a feeling of connection.

As I've found out when speaking with women about their romantic relationships, one of their key desires is to have deeper intimacy with their man. This is true across the range of relationship types and lengths, from newly dating to 20 years married. Her desire for more intimacy doesn't go away, regardless of the number of years a couple is together. Early in a relationship, many women take things in their own hands and translate being intimate into having shared interests. They do all sorts of things that they really have no genuine interest in. In my case I went deer hunting, *once*, and took up golf for a few years. I eventually realized I was starving by the seventh hole and had golfed the equivalent of 18 holes by then too. Alas, I love my husband, but golf was not for me.

While she is doing his activities, a woman can also expect her man to do hers. A tit for a tat, so to speak. The problem is while he is doing them, she has her relationship antennas out a mile long reading his every facial expression and nuance. She often mistakes his rejection of the activity with his reaction to her. What he is about in these situations—what he is always about in any situation—is her reaction to life and to him. "Is she happy?" he wonders and worries. Because if he has gone to a dreaded dance class and she is not happy—I really mean to say "delighted"—then there is no way he is going to be happy. Where does this leave men and women with intimacy building? Let's review:

- Girls and then women have more intimate friendship relations versus boys and men
- He wants to win with her, even and especially, in the intimacy area
  (You may be thinking "bedroom" here, which is true, only let's keep to non-physical intimacy.)
- Intimacy is built over time, not purchased, ordered over the internet or made by hand, and that makes it difficult to attain
- Generally speaking, he likely doubts his ability to deliver intimacy, at least until he has a good track record of winning

Therefore, (drum roll please) the woman needs to point out what feels emotionally intimate to her. It is especially important to mention all of the emotional intimacy experiences that do not involve sexual experiences. Many men, and women too, assume all sexual experiences are by default emotionally intimate experiences as well, and the truth is they may not actually be. Then, once the intimacy ball is rolling, she needs to acknowledge her man and praise him while building intimacy with him.

Intimacy Praise Possibilities

Because this is such a loaded area, I want to give women some lines to help encourage and support men in learning how to build intimacy. These phrases are supportive and start like this:

♦ "I felt really close to you when _____."
♦ "I felt deeply connected with you when _____."
♦ "I really felt like we were a team when _____."

Many women are so used to the intimacy dance they do with other women that they are no longer conscious about what they have been doing to build intimacy in their relationships. For women, saying out loud what intimacy-building experiences are might feel like stating the obvious. And yet it probably is not obvious for him. Combining one of the phrases listed above to one of the lines below may bring ideas to mind that she can use. For example, "I really feel close to you when…":

♦ "… when you call me in the middle of your busy day to share something that just happened."
♦ "… when you look deeply in my eyes for a minute."
♦ "…when you put your hand in the small of my back as we stand side-by-side listening to the kids' stories."
♦ "…when you reminisce with me about fun times we've shared."
♦ "…when you share your feelings about how someone is treating you."
♦ "…when you talk to me about ideas and plans you have for us in the future."
♦ "…when you share stories from your family that explain your reaction to things in life now."
♦ "…when you hold my hand in the car driving along or as we walk down the street."
♦ "…when you come up behind me in the kitchen and rub my neck and shoulders."

This list could go on and on. You get the point: there are a million big and little things he has done or can do to build intimacy. Even if he's only done something once, it is a start to building intimacy. He needs you to let him know when it has gone well, when he has done something you liked, when he is winning with you!

The real life version of men and intimacy is quite different than the romance novel version of Romeos who elegantly and gallantly lead the charge. The beautiful truth is that once you get a man going in the emotional intimacy department, he will delight you with as many ways as you will acknowledge and show gratitude for. Over time he will step out on his own to add in some new approaches to intimacy. When he does, give him the win.

SKILL ALERT: Intimate Radar Readings

Given the reality of men and intimacy, be sure some of your Radar Readings include intimacy-building ideas versus only gifts, projects or events. These ideas are simple things that he could surprise you with any day of the week because they don't take loads of time or preparation.

- "The best greeting is a 10-second kiss from you."
- "I'd love a dinnertime story where you tell me a favorite memory you have of me."
- "I feel cared about when you do soft rubs along my arm."
- "I really enjoy it when we read an article in the paper or a magazine together and chat about it."
- "It's fun to share old photos and swap stories."

He Won't Win At "House" (Unless You Let Him)

One of the biggest sources of angst, frustration and anger for the married women I speak with are simple household tasks that go unnoticed by her man or are not done to her standards. Quite honestly, the house is a mine field for men. There are so many ways for him to lose! Male readers are nodding right now. It is the women readers who have likely never considered their house in quite this way.

Why is this? A little history review may be helpful. The documentary *Miss Representation*, by Jennifer Siebel Newsom, highlights that after World War II ended the men came home and needed jobs. Many women were immediately laid off. Advertising campaigns for new appliances were employed to entice women back into the homes to free up the jobs for men.

In the 1950s young women took home economics classes to accumulate skills towards fulfilling the "housewife" role. Images in popular women's magazine show pictures of women in the kitchen or women serving food to her husband, in a dress and heels. When we see those images now, we laugh at the absurdity. Back then it was normal.

Later, in 1962 an organization called Catalyst opened its doors with a novel idea: they approached high school girls to encourage them to work part-time before having children. In that era, while some girls were going to college, most still had the idea that they would ultimately be housewives. For those of us who grew up in the 1970s or earlier, the house was the woman's domain. Our well meaning mothers passed along all of their household tips, either overtly or covertly, just as their mothers had for them. Passing along of household knowledge is a multi-generational tradition.

One Right Way Myth

In my case I learned that there is a proper way to put the toilet paper roll on the holder (end hangs over the top), how to fold the towels (thirds, not in half), how to load the dishwasher properly (silverware handles up, not down), the correct way to make a bed corner (military style) or how to fold the dreaded bottom sheet (create a square). There was one right way to do these things and I learned it. My two brothers were not on the same program. A progressive woman, my mom expected them to do laundry, change their sheets and even clean their bathroom. The rigor with which they had to perform these tasks was at a different level for obvious reasons. My brothers were possibly going to be "helping" their spouse whereas I was going to be the chief person in charge of the house. There was no lecture on this. That was just the way it was. My brothers, and most men of that era and before, did not get the same household training as their female sibling(s) and counterparts. Beyond my mother, other women helped make sure I would be well trained. When I was in middle school my mother arranged for me to clean one of her friend's houses, an optometrist's wife who also worked in his office. One day my mom told me I had to return to the house because I hadn't cleaned the bathroom sink properly and her friend was going to instruct me. Add "right way to clean a sink" to my list.

Oddly girls growing up in other households learned different methods. For example, my mother-in-law has her toilet paper rolls the opposite of mine. (Yes, it takes all of my willpower to not reverse them for her.) If there is only one way to do something, then how could a towel not be folded in thirds or the toilet paper be put on "backwards" at someone else's house? That is my point. Many women, me included, have a definite way to do things around the house. Her approach may have been ingrained in her growing up, or it is the way she now prefers. Does this ring a bell for you? Take a moment to mentally list out a few of the household tasks that have a definite way they need to be done or a definite order for doing them. All of these "definites" represent a land mine for a man. The truth is—*sorry Mom*—there is more than one way to do anything around the house. Often a man does not experience that there are many ways to do accomplish tasks around his house. There is one way, his wife or partner's way, and he is not doing it that way. He is doing it "wrong."

What is fascinating to me is that I do not have the same standards for the yard work as I do for housework. I was a girl treated to mowing the lawn, edging (unfortunately we had an edger) and once the Weed Eater was invented, weed eating. Prior to that we used hand clippers. These tasks were not occasional tasks for me. Raised by an accountant father, we were required to earn money to pay for our clothes and activities. Mowing the yard was worth $15. So was cleaning the house. I did both jobs. My brothers never touched the house jobs, already wise to the pitfalls, no doubt. To this day when company is coming, I rush to the guest bathroom to clean up a ring in the toilet while Clint inspects the yard for any signs of work needed. What's odd is that on an ongoing basis, we both do indoor and outdoor tasks around our house. We even have a weekly list to divvy the tasks up so no one is stuck with the same job repetitively. The weekly task list also ensures our daughter learns and contributes to a variety of household chores, inside and out. Truth be told, I want to make sure she has an expectation that she will share household tasks with her life partner and any children they have, because without divvying them up, she is still the most likely candidate to be trapped in the traditional "housewife" role.

Right Or Happy?

What do we do about all of this housewife history and these stereotypical roles, which sometimes aren't so stereotypical after all? As in all areas of life, a man needs to win at home in order to be motivated and engaged at home. A woman's solution for him, and for her ultimate happiness and peace of mind, is to let him win. After all, men put their attention where they are winning. He can do household chores without winning. My husband did that for years. The pace was slow. His attitude was sluggish. I was looking over his shoulder to offer suggestions or even teach him what to do. He really didn't seem that interested in my incredible wealth of domestic knowledge. This bugged me. I wasn't happy. I guess you already know from the previous chapter that he wasn't happy either. Many men are not happy as they contemplate household projects, even the ones that use skills they enjoy such as building and carpentry. A girlfriend's husband explained it this way to one of his buddies:

> "I have some projects to do this weekend and I'm
> not looking forward to them. I know at some point
> I'm going to do something wrong. I don't know
> what it will be this time. If I knew what it was, I
> wouldn't do it. But I don't."

No man signs up eagerly for a losing situation. It goes against his core desire to win. Since men put their attention where they are winning, he needs to win at home before he's going to happily put his attention there. Does this mean he will become a domestic god? Not likely! I have to tell you, it is pretty nice to be married to a man who does laundry when the basket is gets full, empties the dishwasher when the clean light is on, wipes off counters, cleans the sink at the end of the night, clears the old food out of the refrigerator, sorts and puts mail away, wipes the water around the edges of the bathroom sink…and on and on—all with no prompting and a lot of gratitude after the fact from me.

Early in our marriage I fell into how to have a partner around my house who feels equally vested in the various household tasks versus a "helper" in my home, who occasionally lends a hand when I point something out. Clint had a laundry incident and I accidentally responded in a way that he did get criticized for, which he would experience as a "loss." (That story in a moment.) Recently I had another opportunity to revisit a choice that for me underlies the household struggles that many women in my workshops report experiencing with their men: Do I want to be right or do I want to be happy? When it comes to men winning in the house with household tasks, this is the only question you must answer. Candidly, the right-or-happy question applies to nearly any situation between a man and a woman in relationship. For now, we'll stick with the house.

Shrunken Sweater Story

When we were first married, I knew that I did not want all of the jobs around my house that my mom had around her house. My dad was born in the 1930s and to this day has no idea how to start a dishwasher, a washing machine or even the toaster oven. Not long into our marriage, Clint washed a load of clothes and then came to me with a doll-sized version of the wool sweater my mom had worn in high school and had passed along to me. It was a vintage piece of clothing and one I treasured. Clint had put it in the drier. For non-laundry readers, driers shrink wool, at least the old wool that clothes used to be made from in the 1950s. Clint felt awful because he knew a bit about the history of the sweater. He asked if there was any way to fix it. I like to believe that my higher self stepped in to save me that day. Perhaps it was simply that I was still running on newlywed energy. I was actually gracious. There was no "How could you?" No tears. No ridiculing phone calls that he could overhear to lament with girlfriends. I looked at that sweater and thought, "I can either be afraid of all of the other pieces of clothing he might ruin, and thus never let him do the laundry again, or I can sacrifice the sweater, and whatever other garments he might ruin, and not have the job for my entire life." We were in our 20's at the time, so I figured I had a good 50+ years of laundry duty ahead. I did not make the sweater incident a huge crime. As a result, Clint made it a huge learning experience. Anytime he had any doubt about how to wash any piece of my clothing, he brought it to me to ask. He still does.

Ultimately I shared the story of the sweater with my friends. So many women admitted that they do not allow their boyfriends or husbands to touch their laundry. They wondered how I could. "What if he ruins something else?" I reminded them that it is clothing, an inanimate object. I intended my marriage to outlive my clothing. I also secretly wondered to myself how they could sign up for a life sentence of laundry.

Shower Cleaner or Great Husband?

With the economic downturn in 2009, my financial industry speaking engagements and consulting came to an abrupt halt. As I reinvented my work, I suggested we could save money by cleaning our own house. Plus, our daughter, who had been treated to professional cleaning her entire life, could learn some of the skills. It would be good for her. (Yes, I admit the generational passing along of household cleaning knowledge was also at hand. I knew that if she lived in a dirty house, she would be judged for it more than her male partner.) We made a list of all of the cleaning tasks and decided which needed to be done weekly and which could be done every other week. Our master bathroom shower hit the twice-a-month list, which seemed appropriate. However, our family was not running a cleaning business, so in reality not all of the tasks were done to the schedule. That meant that sometimes the shower was cleaned only once a month, and with that timing the grout actually began getting traces of some pink, living organism. (Gross, I know.)

Several times Clint cleaned the shower after our pink guests had begun to appear. The problem was that after his cleaning there was still some areas that had algae. The first time or two I simply caught those areas while I was showering. Over time, I got more and more miffed about it. (In the *He's Not Broken* chapter I explore why a small thing can set a woman off. Read ahead if you need to explore this idea now.) What to do? I knew Clint needed to win in order to stick with the home cleaning project. He wasn't that thrilled about it in the first place. I, on the other hand, was committed to demonstrating to our daughter that both women and men participate equally in domestic chores. Once again I think I was saved by my higher self. Just as I had decided that I was going to say something about it, it dawned on me that Clint likely wasn't missing some of the pink areas on purpose. He wasn't doing a poor job to bug me or test me. I recalled that prior to our marriage he and his male roommates shared their shower with some very odd-colored algae, though I knew he'd outgrown bachelor-style living. Most likely he did not want to shower in a pink shower either.

SKILL ALERT: The Benefit Of The Doubt Rule

I decided to extend him "The Benefit of the Doubt Rule." You have likely heard this old adage. This rule is something we instituted in our marriage early on and it has served us all of these years. We agreed that I love Clint immensely and he loves me just as much. Can you hear newlyweds proclaiming this? Regardless of how long you have been together or married, a pledge of your love is possible. Therefore, coming from a place of love, we would not *choose* to intentionally do something annoying or hurtful to one another. That does not mean that we would not actually end up doing something hurtful or annoying. It is for times when feathers are ruffled or feelings are hurt that the rule comes in. Whenever Clint does something that is annoying or has hurt my feelings, before I react harshly, I institute The Benefit of the Doubt Rule. For the times when I forget to institute it before reacting, Clint can institute it on his own behalf by asking for "the benefit of the doubt." In either case, once The Benefit of the Doubt Rule is in play, I remind myself that Clint loves me and would not do something awful intentionally. Therefore, there must be something else going on, something that I do not yet see or understand.

When I instituted this rule during the shower incident, I realized he couldn't see the leftover algae. His eye sight is not as good as mine. He was, in fact, cleaning the shower to the best of his ability. Beyond that, he was expecting a win for his efforts. I asked myself, "Carolyn, do you want to be married to a man who can clean the shower proficiently or do you want him to be great as a husband, a father and in his career?" This question, by the way, is a different version of "Do you want to be right or do you want to be happy?" Both versions are effective for me. I decided the great husband/great dad version of Clint was far more important to me that the pink-algae-cleaning version of him. In case you are wondering what I did about the pink algae, I simply made sure that we kept to the schedule a bit better when it came to the shower task. Also, since the jobs rotated, if it had been a long time between cleanings, I suggested our daughter or I take the shower task that week. There is always more than one way to clean house.

He's Not Broken

I have become convinced there is a fear that unconsciously rattles through a woman when she is in a relationship with a man. It is like a low-grade virus that is always present, sometimes flairs up and never completely goes away. This fear has many versions, though the underlying worry is: is my man broken, defective or lacking in some fundamental way? (Flair ups about this question, by the way, often happen as a woman talks to her girlfriends about her man. Be careful!)

Brain Fear

Most women do not think about this in a conscious, straightforward manner, nor ponder it aloud. Actually, it is much more subtle than that. I believe it is a primal idea hidden in the recesses of the reptilian brain, the part of the brain that is forever assessing for danger. Its sole job is to store information that can protect us from perceived or real danger in the future. In this case, the brain's question is, "Am I safe with this man?" Safety, I believe, goes beyond physical safety to emotional safety and to financial security over a lifetime together.

Sheila's Story

It does not matter whether a woman is just starting to date

or whether she has been married for over 20 years like my client Sheila. As I was writing this book, I began offering the *He's Not Your Girlfriend Mini Series*. Sheila was in my first class and shared this story several months after taking it:

> "Tim and I have some friends that we visit and eat dinner with two to three times a week. Recently we were going to have a party at our house, and I mentioned to Tim that I was going to borrow our friends' 3-tiered tray. Tim didn't recall the tray, so I pointed out that it sits on their breakfast bar counter and has for the past few years. Still no recall. I described it in detail. Nothing. I explained again exactly where it sits on the counter. It was clear he had no idea what I was talking about."

Sheila felt triumphant when she remembered, "He's not my girlfriend!" Because of course any of Sheila's girlfriends would have spotted the piece and known what she was referring to. She also admitted that before taking my class, she would have stewed for days, weeks and even months about Tim's inability to recall the 3-tiered tray. "I would have been so upset about the tray, and he would have been 'losing' with me." What Sheila shared next was even more revealing about where women's thoughts go: "I found myself wondering, 'If he's missed this simple, 3-tiered tray over the past few years, what other, bigger things has he missed'?" Sheila took an innocent experience and associated a bigger meaning to it.

She Extrapolates

That's what women do. Our minds are active and we

envision multiple scenarios. We extrapolate. We do it in countless ways. Here are some of my around-the-house examples:

♦ "If he can't even wipe up the mess on the edges of the sink …"

♦ "If he can't get our daughter started on her bedtime routine …"

♦ "If he can't remember how much I admired the _____ and know I'd like it for my birthday…"

The bottom line on all of this is: If I can't trust him with the little things, how can I trust him with the big things? The truth is Tim is quite capable of noticing the 3-tiered tray. He doesn't choose to. Nor has he or his friends been trained to, in most cases, by his male culture. It helps to see that the reverse is true for women. Many men in North American have an amazing ability to recite sports box scores and recall previous sporting events, including scoring details and key plays. Some do it for one sport. Some do it for many sports. (Yes, there are some men who do not follow sports nor keep track of these statistics. I have spoken with them and it can be very difficult for them to relate to other men in social settings.) In this case, Sheila conceded Tim follows sports and knows his statistics on them. I asked her if she knew any of the recent scores or sports statistics. "Nope—not one." I then asked her if she had to, could she learn them. "Of course!" I bet you know where we are headed here. Not knowing the sports scores does not alter Sheila's capabilities as a person, a woman, a wife, a worker or a mother. She simple doesn't choose to put her focus there. Likewise, Tim not noticing their friends' 3-tiered tray does not alter his capabilities as a person, a man, a husband, a worker or a father.

Yes, but…Already a woman's mind is off to the races with the "Yes, buts":

- ♦ "Yes, but if he isn't able to do two things at once, how can I trust him to look after the children?"
- ♦ "Yes, but if he doesn't notice the broken toilet handle, how can I rely upon him for the bigger issues?"
- ♦ "Yes, but if he doesn't take care of himself when he is sick, how will I know he can take care of me?"
- ♦ "Yes, but if he doesn't remember to call his mom, is he going to be a good lifelong companion for me?"

Now we are getting to the roots of the fear and where it takes women. A missed 3-tier tray is used as a clue, and often an indictment, about his abilities elsewhere. Women begin looking for other evidence, other clues. She begins noticing where he is wrong. I'm not saying this is conscious. This is the subtlest of subtle. The only clue is when a woman gets upset over a small, inanimate object and she is sure she is right: "He should have noticed the 3-tiered tray after all of these years!" When women are taking this stance, we are right and we are not happy. That is the real clue.

Culture Matters

Beyond gender culture there are other cultures at play. In North America I mentioned men are trained to remember box scores and key plays, while women are oriented to remember tiered trays, other decorations and how someone is dressed. Is that all there is to it? No. We couldn't cover all there is to it, though we ought to cover a couple of key areas: cultural heritage and family culture. While I have facilitated a range of diversity training sessions, I am not an expert in all varieties of diversity and all of the subcultures in the U.S. and in families. You, however, are an expert in yours, so take a moment to see what rings true for you while I take a moment to share an eye-opening experience I had with my niece and an African American girlfriend of mine that took place over lunch one day:

> My 15-year-old niece was visiting and my girlfriend, who was also raising a daughter, started asking her what she wanted to do in her life. My niece replied that she planned to become a kindergarten teacher as a hobby and then get married and stay home with babies. My girlfriend, April, asked her what she would do if she wasn't happily married and needed to get a divorce. How would she support herself? My niece had no answers.

What April and I discussed later is that in her culture many women have been raised to not depend upon men. A man may not be there for a woman. Thus, her girl was being raised to be independent and rely upon herself. Meanwhile my niece had more of the knight-in-shining-armor idea of men. Indeed her mom, a highly accomplished business woman, often joked about marrying a wealthy man to take care of her—a financial crutch she actually didn't need. The problem was my niece had already bought into that fantasy.

Another client of mine admitted that her parents were divorced when she was young and her mother, struggling to raise the family on her own, was bitter. She never remarried, and she did not trust men. This set up a pattern of her mother, wanting to protect her daughter from the pain she had experienced, pointing out how wrong men are and how they cannot be trusted. My client realized she had continued with her mother's perspective into her own marriage.

What programming did you get at home? What came to you as part of your ethnic culture? These lenses are what women see men through, even if the women did not consciously choose these perspectives. These inherited ideas keep women's reptilian brains alert, ever vigilant for clues about men. From there, women extrapolate. One missed 3-tiered tray becomes an indictment. As Sheila knew, and you may have already experienced, this does not lead to marital bliss or shared joy. There is a better way.

Part III

Reality Check!

He's A Lot Of Overhead

This chapter title reflects my initial thought about investing time and energy into understanding my husband's needs and responding to him differently in our marriage. Other women in my workshops have mirrored this concern, either in their words, their looks or their sighs. The truth is a woman can "do" her life and all of the tasks in her life herself, even when she is in a committed relationship or marriage. Many women do. As you may have surmised from the stories I've shared, I have been "Wonder Woman" in my marriage. Over time, I found it exhausting to run the show and I also found it lonely. I didn't get married to live that way.

As good as our relationship already was, I guess a part of me knew that there was more to experience—the next level, if you will. This book is an invitation for you to understand your man in a deeper way. You can step into some new approaches that honor both of you so you can experience each other differently. One of the women who participated in the *He's Not Your Girlfriend Mini Series* shared her reaction to the tips and tools she learned during the workshop in the email below. In it she describes the attitude many women have towards their partners. She also addresses why she chooses to put her effort into her husband:

"For me, one of the most powerful/motivating things you said during the course was something to the effect of...if you do this "relationship work," (be generous with approval, notice his sensitivity, give

him ways to "win," etc.), you will be rewarded with a more intimate, connected relationship. That's what I'm going for. That's definitely what I want! I have to say....I feel a number of my girlfriends would just groan/sigh at the idea of putting this kind of effort into their marriages/relationships. It's like they are willing to kill themselves for their kids, their jobs, but (apart from an occasional "date night"), they really don't want to change their behavior or adopt new practices that might actually enhance their relationships with their husbands/partners. I feel that's so sad. And kind of scary. Maybe it's because it took me so long to find the right man for me (unlike many of my girlfriends) that I just really want my relationship to be fantastic!"

When I first taught relationship workshops I excitedly recruited couples and they responded, "We are not having any problems." When it comes to relationships, we operate more on a "break-fix" mentality. Even at that, couples too often only exert extra effort on their relationship when things are dire and often beyond fixing. It's as if we are stuck in the taboo around relationships work left over from the 1960s. I naively thought that people would happily want to maintain and improve their relationships—regardless of how good they already were—just as Clint and I had done. In North America we seem committed to preventative maintenance in many areas of life. Why not relationship maintenance? We regularly maintain our cars, our yards, our homes, our clothing and our health. Frequently we invest a lot of time or money (or both) on these maintenance areas. I am encouraging you to add relationship maintenance to the mix as well. The rewards are phenomenal and it's more fun than pulling weeds! Plus, an improved relationship will enhance your entire life.

Why Bother? I Can Do It Myself

By now there is a distinct possibility that some of the other "Wonder Women" reading this book are thinking:

Wait, I'm supposed to turn my life over to him and be willing to wait forever for him to kick into gear? Then I'm supposed to be profusely supportive and, later still, grateful? All the while I could be doing things just the way I want them, when I want them. I don't think so!

I'll be the first to admit that at a blush this doesn't seem like a very good tradeoff. The key word here is "I." As in you, alone, handling your life. Your man will let you do that, and he may put his attention elsewhere, where he can win. I admit for many of our house projects I could easily go to Home Depot (once), get the parts and do the project myself. But, I recognize this is a double-edged sword. I can do it my way and not engage my husband. Then I have all the jobs, and that leads to resentment. I certainly have been there. Have you seen resentment in a relationship? Resentment is an ugly cancer that creeps into every crevice and takes a tenacious hold. I want all women to avoid resentment at all costs.

There are two ways to look at it. The first is I have all the jobs so they will be done exactly my way and done exactly when I want them done. Or the alternative is I engage my man and take on the role of acknowledging and appreciating him. In the latter, my experience is fuller and my man is happier. When

I stop giving him my advice and suggestions, my husband usually delivers in a much bigger way than I had ever envisioned. He often goes one step further towards delighting me with the end result, and he does it in ways I had not thought of. There is an upside to this approach. It is not just that I get what I want. I get *more* than I wanted, and I have an eager partner. Actually, we had been married 15 years when I finally realized, "Oh my goodness! I have this huge partner in my life, called my husband, whom I haven't been engaging fully for the first 15 years of our marriage." It was such a delight to turn him on. (Not sexually, though this supportive approach also applies in that arena too.) It felt as if I literally flipped the switch from "off" to "on" by involving him in handling the big and small details in our life. That is not to say that I don't sometimes find myself taking stuff back—old habits die hard! I might think, "Oh, this will be great," as I handle whatever project I had the idea about. Now I often have a new thought. I think, "Wow, that's too bad. I took from him. I took the possibility of winning." I actually took from myself too. I could have had an even better outcome.

He's So Sensitive

As I was explaining to my girlfriend how I was going to go about the boat date idea I covered in an earlier chapter, she commented about how surprised she was that men need so much reinforcement. She wondered why I couldn't just say, "Oh that's great. We're on the boat. You bought a bottle of champagne. Thank you." This is what women often do. We treat our men in the way we need to be treated. Generally speaking a simple thank you works for a woman and her girlfriends. Remind yourself, "He is not me." A man needs to win with his woman. Any indicator she can give him that he's winning, and as often as she can give it to him, is valuable. Give him the win as often as you can. I think you will find that he will strive for your happiness and his future wins even more.

Another thing women fail to recognize is that men are sensitive. Men certainly underestimate their level of sensitivity because the male culture teaches them that to be a man is to be independent, strong and handle life on his own. I teach that men are more sensitive than women. Shocking? It is for most people until they look a little closer and discover it's true. First let's look at women. Before reading further, think of the ways that women demonstrate sensitivity. Here are a few common ones:

- Women often announce "my feelings got hurt"
- Women's eyes readily tear up or they cry (for a number of reasons, including anger)
- Women use a tone of voice that conveys their feeling
- Women inquire about other's feelings, "Are you upset?"
- Women talk about their own feelings
- Women validate other's feelings, "I know how you feel…"
- Women seek out emotion-laden entertainment (e.g. books, movies, workshops)

There are lots of clues women give off about their sensitivity. How do we know when men are sensitive or when they have hurt feelings? Well, once again, this is an area where he's not like your girlfriend. Remember he didn't play with dolls; he played competition. Competition encourages boys to use a "game face" which can hide what he really feels. "I've got this handled," is what the game face says. Beyond sports, there is the One-Upmanship game which teaches boys and men to put on a tough exterior. Men may keep their reactions and emotions hidden because they do not want to be called a sissy, a wimp or worse. Often a common response for boys and men is "I'll show you. In the next competition or next time we banter, I'll get you back. I'm not going to show how much this hurt; however, I will get you back."

Given all of this is it any wonder that men are not characterized as sensitive? I believe men and women have become immune to noticing men's sensitivity. Most women do not know how to honor a man's sensitivity. In the *He's Not Your Girlfriend Mini Series* workshop I share examples of how I notice Clint's sensitivity. Every man is different. It is important for a woman to learn to spot her man's signs of sensitivity. On a day-in, day-out basis he is not going to tear up or have a conversation with her about how she hurt his feelings. I believe women hurt men's feeling all of the time, and women don't even know they are doing it. When I hurt Clint's feelings, he's doesn't give off the same clues my girlfriends would. In the workshop I encourage participants to spend a week looking for signs of sensitivity in the men they encounter. I encourage you to do the same. Discover, first of all, is it true that men are sensitive? And, if so, how does it show up? Before sharing my viewpoint, mentally list a few ways can you think of that men show sensitivity. In my experience, men's sensitive responses include:

- ♦ Men get defensive
- ♦ Men have an odd reaction to a comment
- ♦ Men show women what they have accomplished

♦ Men turn off or shut down

The first thing I notice with Clint around sensitivity is defensiveness. This isn't surprising. After all, in sports often times the best offense is a good defense. One night Clint asked me how a *He's Not Your Girlfriend Mini Series* call had gone. I began sharing with him the list we had generated of all the ways that men can lose around the house. The entire time I was speaking about and referring to the call, only Clint translated my conversation about the call to a conversation about him. At first I didn't realize what had happened because I was speaking about the call. All of a sudden Clint defensively began taking me through the list of things he had done that night around the house, "I cooked the dinner, I did the dishes and I washed down the counters." I recall thinking, "What does that have to do with my call?" When a man reacts by listing all of the things he has done or is doing, his defensiveness is a clue. By the way, when I detect defensiveness with Clint I don't say, "Uh oh, I hurt your feelings." The first thing any man would say is, "No you didn't." I understand something is awry through his defensive response, not his verbal expression of hurt feelings. Perhaps a better way to think about a defensive response is, "Uh oh, he's not winning with me." Even if I have no idea why he isn't winning, his listing off of accomplishments is a clue. Now I realize that he is so far from winning with me that he's pointing out all the areas he should be getting a win.

Another way men let us know they are sensitive to how much they are winning is that they take us on a tour of their accomplishments. When Clint has finished trimming the yard, he takes me on a tour. If I don't notice something, he points it out "Look over there. Look at the rose bush I trimmed up." In my workshops I can almost see light bulbs go off for women who have also experienced their man pointing out the work he has done. He is looking for the win, without perhaps even knowing it himself. Before I understood this dynamic I was annoyed with these tours. Other women report this to me as well. Now I have fun on them. I reply, "Oh honey, you did. It looks great." After all, we are in love with these men, so to have them feel great, to find something that easily lifts them up and motivates them to do more, is easily worth it.

Another clue about sensitivity can be an odd response in a conversation. The other night the buzzer went off for the fish we had baking in the oven. Clint asked me to check it. When I got to the oven I noticed that it was set on the convection setting, not the regular setting, which means it would cook faster, so I said to him, "Oh, the oven is on convection so I'm sure it's done." What Clint heard is, "The oven is on the wrong setting." He started explaining to me that everyone is doing the best job they can do. I thought, "What does that have to do with the fish being done?" I realized once again how sensitive he is. What he heard is, "You did it wrong." My comment was not a judgment about his cooking skills. I was simply expressing my surety that the fish was done. The truth is, I didn't even know who had started the oven—Clint, my daughter or me. Now when I get an odd reaction I ask myself, "Is he losing with me?" This question often helps me realize that what I said versus what he heard may be two very different things. I recognize he may not be winning with me.

Another area of sensitivity can arise during a project as I (a.k.a. The Improvement Queen) offer suggestions. If Clint shuts down or has an attitude shift, this is my clue. I already shared quit a bit about this dynamic in the Retiring The Improvement Queen chapter, though it's important enough to review again briefly. Even though I teach this, recently I almost set myself up by making a suggestion when Clint was in the midst of replacing a light switch. As his screwdriver kept slipping, it looked to me like the screwdriver he was using was too big for the light switch plate screw. It took everything in me not to tell him he needed a smaller screwdriver. If it had been one of my girlfriends, I would have told her and she probably would have agreed. As I have already shared, with Clint I might hear, "Whatever you want." Or his attitude will shift. I used to get angry. I finally realized that what he hears in my suggestions is, "You are doing it wrong." He's doing the project thinking he's going to get a win, and he's actually getting a loss along the way. Men have sensitivity to suggestions, even simple ones like using a different screwdriver. My best remedy for Clint's sensitivity is to keep my ideas to myself and take delight in the idea that he is delivering the project instead of me.

The truth is a man is more sensitive than he lets on. His sensitivity is why winning with his woman is so important. Sensitivity is why he often sputters as he contemplates a project and doubts himself. He needs support and encouragement. Too often his woman mistranslates sputtering as reluctance or complaining and she stomps off to do the project herself, as I used to do. Sensitivity is why a man takes his woman on a tour after a project is completed so he can be acknowledged and get a win with her. Ultimately a man's sensitivity is a good thing—it drives his desire to deliver missions and win with the woman he loves.

He May Need Resuscitating

From my teaching I recognize there is a broad range of relationship experiences and histories. For those currently in a relationship, what have you two lived through? When you step back and assess things, has he been wining? Has she shown him her gratitude and happiness?

For people with perfectionist tendencies like mine, it may be easy to "awfulize" what is going on in your relationship relative to the new ideas and approaches shared here. It is not fair to hold your past history up for scrutiny against a new standard, so please don't. (I promised no guilt trips in the Three Ways To Read This Book section and I meant it.) Such relationship scrutiny would be like expecting yourself to win a game of chess before you had ever learned to play. Hard to do. My experience is that every couple has some of what I teach going on somewhere in their relationship: she notices, he attempts to delight her, she thanks him or she allows him to do projects his own way. There is something going right for everyone, even if it is only in small doses or discreet areas.

The trick now is to identify a few places to gain some momentum. Whatever your feeling about your relationship, please know men are amazingly resilient. Their competitive environments teach them that one loss does not make for a season of losses. In baseball, for example, a man may not have gotten a hit for the last 10 at bats, yet he will stand there again, believing this is the time. When he steps up to the plate, his teammates cheer him on. They know he will do it eventually and they all hope this is the time (because, of course, they want to win). He gets strength from their cheers. A woman has this same opportunity to cheer her man on as he steps up to the plate to deliver for her again. He may be a bit leery. He may need to pile up a few good wins before his confidence is restored and he is willing to take a risk by going for a big "homerun swing," if you will. How many wins? How much time will this take? I don't know. I encourage women to start in small ways. Start with lots of NAGing (Notice, Acknowledge, Gratitude). One of my clients said she was going to "Appreciate at least one thing per day. If I can do that, in a year that is 365 times I get to say something nice to him. That will be a very powerful change in our total pattern of communication." Indeed, that is a powerful start—for both of them.

What About Me & My Needs?

As you've experienced, this book is about what makes men tick in relationships. However, this is not to imply that women don't have needs as well. Yes we do—lots of them! It would take several volumes and a lifetime to explain women, so believe me when I say this is a very brief overview of a few key needs for women in romantic relationships. Many of these needs Eva and Will highlight and go into great detail in their workshop. Others I have confirmed and added from my gender work, consulting experiences and relationship workshops. I have already mentioned that most men are honest in stating that they do not understand women. Thank goodness they are willing to try to figure them out! What I have not stated is that women often believe they know so much about themselves in relationships. Yet my female clients have the biggest Aha!s when I teach my *What Women Want And How To Get It* workshop. This section is written for women. It is my hope that you will consider the needs I share and see if they are a fit for you. It might also be fun to read this section with your man and notice when he starts nodding.

The beautiful part of relationships is that men are perfectly suited for women. Here's how it works. He makes her happy by meeting her needs. He delights her and she, in turn, compliments and shows gratitude to him. This gives him the win and thus fulfills his biggest need in his relationship. As I have mentioned earlier, women are moving targets. This is true in relationships and in life, in general. This means that just as a man figures out one way to please a woman, she will come up with a new need. While you may have a million different needs, there are some basics that most women want with their men and in their life.

Attention Please!

If a man's number one need is to win and receive gratitude, then a woman's is for attention. The good news is that attention can take many forms. One of the primary ways a woman feels she is getting attention is when her man listens to her. This can be extremely challenging for him as women and men have very different communication styles, which we've already touched upon. Men are direct, to the point, logical and often succinct. Women circle around a topic, take segues and pile on bundles of details. That can result in the glazed look of an overwhelmed man now victim to "TMI" (too much information). I used to teach that women say three times as many words as men. As I was writing this book I was surprised to discover that this is a stereotype. Updated research, reported on by NPR (All Things Considered, July 5, 2007), shows that men and women actually use about the same number of words a day, contrary to previous assertions. (When I shared this update with Clint, he flatly refused to believe it. Based on his experience, he says he's holding out for further research.) Regardless of what research discovers about the number of words each gender uses, there are differences in the content of the conversations. I believe it is the style of a woman's conversation that makes it hard for him to stay with her through the entire conversation.

This is why many men have adopted the phrases, "Uh huh," "Really," and "You're kidding me" to feign interest while tuning out.

Beyond communication style differences, there are other attention stealers. For years I told my family and anyone who would listen to me, that I hated television. I resented the countless hours of sports parading through my living room. There was always some "big game" that I felt less important than. Then one day I woke up to the reality that my resentment was based upon my unmet need for the attention that television was stealing from me. I was competing with an inanimate object and it felt demeaning. I actually like television and can become extremely engrossed in a show. Beyond television, many women complain about their men's hobbies. When I hear a woman making this complaint I think two things, "She may not be getting the attention she needs and so she resents the hobby." The second thing I think is, "He may not be winning with her so he's put his attention to his hobby." Are you competing for attention with a hobby?

Variety—The Spice for Women

People say, "Variety is the spice of life," and women seem to live this saying. It is certainly true in my life. I don't like to eat the same foods two days in a row. I don't like to go on the same vacations year after year. I don't like to drive the same way to work each day. I don't like to go on the same date or to the same restaurant over and over again. I like to mix it up. The truth is I do not know what is going to be the winning mix tomorrow, let alone next week. Neither does my husband.

It is important for men to know that generally speaking women like variety. We like it in all things: food, sex, clothing, dates, activities, and friends. The problem is that once a man gets a win in one way, he is tempted to continue delivering that same thing. It's a sure win. The more confident he is from continually winning with her and the more she NAGs him—the Notice, Acknowledge, Gratitude version—the more willing he will be to continually mix it up. This becomes a win-win for both of them.

Keep Me Safe

When I traveled the country as a keynote speaker and trainer for financial advisors on how to work with women, I learned firsthand how important security is to women. In study after study women rated security as their number one need financially. Shockingly, a Goldman Sachs survey of women with a net worth of over $5,000,000 (yes, five million dollars, this is not a typo) revealed that their number one fear is that they will become bag ladies! (*Really?!*) Even at this level of financial success, their need for security outweighed all other options. (Source: Selling Your Toughest Customer workshop). Beyond financial security, I have found women also want to feel they are generally safe. This includes those elements on Maslow's hierarchy of needs—food, shelter, protection from danger—and goes beyond them, into emotional safety with her man. Emotional safety is probably best left to psychologist and psychiatrists. For our purposes, emotional safety covers the gamut from not being ridiculed, demeaned or degraded on the negative end of the range to being uplifted, supported and loved on the positive end of the range.

Adore Me

One of the many ways my husband creates that important feeling of emotional security for me is he serenades me every day. Sometimes in big ways and other times in small ways. It is a perfect fit for me. Adoration is a perfect fit for any woman. To the outside world I come off as a confident, I-will-do-anything woman. He knows the softer side of me, the side that needs reassurance. My insecure side wants to know there is a safe space to crawl back to and an adoring man when I get there. Adoration can take so many different forms: words, actions or a combination. For me, each morning when we wake up we have a cuddle session. This is not sex. (Well, mostly not.) During this time he reminds me how happy he is to be married to me. Every single day, without fail he tells me this. Later, when he phones me, he greets me with, "Hello Gorgeous!" or "Hi Beautiful!" To be seen as attractive by her mate is healing for women because we are often very critical of ourselves and our looks. Indeed we have had many years of practice (10,000 hours?). Through my U & Me Camp for Moms and their teen/tween girls, I have discovered this self criticism regarding looks is in full swing by the time girls are in adolescence. My husband is the one I want to hear how beautiful I am from. It literally lights me up inside.

When I phone him, he always tells me how happy he is to hear my voice on the other end of the phone and how he's already looking forward to being together in the evening. In the midst of writing this book, I chanced upon a voicemail that he left me on a day when he was tied up in meetings before we planned to meet for lunch. I thought it might be interesting for you to hear what a healthy, motivated man actually sounds like when adoring his wife:

"Hello Gorgeous Wife. I was thinking of you on a little break. I have to go back [to his meeting] at 11, so I just wanted to tell you how much I love you. I miss you. I think you are the greatest. I miss your smile. I like seeing it. It seems like I've been seeing it a lot lately which is so nice. Okay. See you soon Beautiful One. Bye."

At dinner, he asks about my day and he listens (!) to all of the details. He notices and thanks me for anything I have done for our household, such as emptying the dishwasher, buying groceries or walking the dog. When we go to bed at night, he reminds me again why he's so happy being married to me. It's lovely. When I stay up later than he is doing projects, he comes and finds me and shares his loving words. He also leaves a small light on in our bedroom and turns back my side of the bed to welcome me when I arrive. As you may have read in the Acknowledgements section of the book, Clint has lived with me through my journey to understand gender differences, make peace with them, speak about them, teach them in workshops and then ultimately incorporate them into all aspects of our lives, including our marriage. He has been experimented on. He has attended workshops. He has allowed me to share stories about him in this book (which sets him up for future ribbing). In short, he has been committed to doing and learning whatever it takes to help me be happy along this journey, and I am the happy and grateful recipient of his commitment. His loving gestures mean so much to me. They surround my day from beginning to end and even in-between. As you have already guessed, I am incredibly grateful. I tell him all the time. And the best part is we are engaged in a mutual adoration cycle. I highly recommend it!

"He's *Not* Doing What I Asked!"

The title for this chapter came directly from one of my clients, Beth, who called after taking my *He's Not Your Girlfriend Mini Series* workshop. Beth reported that she wasn't getting results with her husband. Does this happen? Absolutely…and there is usually a reason why. Let me share a few trouble shooting areas to look at before I share Beth's story.

Is He An Emotionally Healthy Man?

My wish is that all women are in a relationship with an emotionally healthy man. This is not always the case, and it may not be the case for you. I covered this at the start of the book and it bears repeating. An emotionally healthy man is one who is motivated to please the woman in his life, to make her happy. He is a man who wants to win with her. He is a man who responds well to her acknowledgement and gratitude—he smiles or even physically stands taller when he receives her compliments. (I say, "He puffs up.") He may also repeat the behavior he is getting acknowledged for. Remember sometimes an emotionally healthy man has put his attention elsewhere because he has not been winning with the woman in his life. If that is the case with you, please review the chapter *He's A Lot Of Overhead*.

Other men are not emotionally healthy in their lives and in

105

their relationships for a variety of reasons, such as family history, previous emotional wounds they have not healed from or addictions. This book and these tips and practices are not for those men, nor for the women who are in relationships with them. That is beyond my area of expertise. I know several women who, after being in a relationship with an unhealthy man, have used my workshops and materials to learn what is healthy and to heal. It is as if they are doing a reset for what is possible in their romantic lives. I love that!

Has He Been Winning With You?

Winning for a man is like adding gasoline boosters to a car's engine. He perks up and his life runs better. Winning also adds confidence for him to step out and attempt the next new area. If you wonder about this, notice how much your man will repeat something for you that you have shown repeated gratitude for. He'll do it again and again because it is safe and he knows it will make you happy. He is assured a win.

Conversely, if you give a man a new request and he hasn't experienced winning with you very often, he may not feel confident that going down that path will get him, or you, good results. Please note: it does not matter how simple you think the request is. If he's had a past experience with not winning, he may still be gun shy and you don't even recall it. This is particularly true in the household area (as we've already covered in detail in the chapter He Won't Win at House (Unless You Let Him)).

Have You Been Clear?

As I've said, a woman's world operates quite nicely on hints and innuendos. Men do not. While you might think you have been extremely clear about what you want, please take a moment to review in your head if you have let him know clearly or, instead, if you have hinted in a way your girlfriend would understand but your man may not.

Have You Been Too Specific?

Yes, I know this seems to run counter to the previous point. The truth is, though, there is a fine balance between being clear and sending a message that there is only one way to deliver—your way—and there is no room for his approach, his creativity and his ability to wow you.

While you may not have intended it, your request may sound and feel like a demand. Men do not respond well to demands. What he needs is to be pointed in the right direction, not given a step-by-step request. For example, you could say, "I'd like to go on a date where we are outside doing something active like a walk/hike or bike ride or something like that followed by a picnic or some outdoor dining experience. This will be so fun!"

Or you could say, "I'd like to go on a hiking date on the John Muir trail. You can pack us a picnic lunch with ham and cheese and crackers and wine. Oh, and please get the Lindt chocolate with the sea salt that you know I love. This will be so fun!"

They both are polite and nice and express excitement for

what will happen. The second request has most of the details ironed out. There really is no room for him to wow you, and there is a lot of room for him to get it wrong. It almost resembles something that one would have an administrative assistant pull together.

There are typically two reasons women get too specific: 1) based upon past experience, they do not trust their man to deliver; 2) they are being helpful. In both cases there is genuine love going on. She wants him to win with her. It is admirable. Interestingly enough, when we go too far in our specificity, we potentially send him these unintended messages:

- ◆ You are not capable of planning an event with me
- ◆ You and I both know, you have blown it before and you might blow it now
- ◆ You really don't know how to win with me so I have to spell it out

In the end, a woman actually puts more pressure on him because now he is nervous about winning. He's also very aware of all of the ways he could lose. This is a double-whammy-bad combination for a man!

Are You Asking Too Big, Too Soon?

I am absolutely a proponent of a woman asking for what she truly wants versus picking something at the bottom of her Radar Reading that she thinks her man could deliver. Been there, done that. Not satisfying for anyone.

However…a man needs to get some wins, and thus some confidence with her, under his belt before he is ready for the big requests. He needs to have a steady diet of winning with you and winning on the little stuff to be confident to step into the big stuff. Even if you think your request isn't big, it may be in his mind. For a review of this, please return to the chapter *He Wants To Win (Every Time)*.

Beth's Story: "He's *Not* Doing What I Asked!"

Returning to Beth, she and her husband, Jack, actually had several issues going on, which is often the case. She assured me that Jack is a healthy man who is always telling her, "Whatever you want." and "I just want you to be happy." These statements, by the way, are huge clues. In the first situation, she had recently requested that the holiday lights be put up even though there were below freezing temperatures outside and many people in her area had opted to skip lights that year. Her husband braved the weather and made it happen, because he knew the holidays are a big event for Beth. She was thrilled with his results, even though he hadn't yet completed one area that was a bit tricky. When I asked if she had shown gratitude for what he'd done so far, she hadn't. She was waiting to give Jack the big win once all of the lights were completed. I pointed out that there can be more than one win to a single event and that a win in the middle of a project fuels his fire for completion. (This is only true as long as it doesn't include an admonishment for what is missing.) Beth shared that she was worried if she gave Jack the win, he'd stop with the project incomplete. Not so. She agreed to begin giving Jack a win for the lights.

Beth's other issue was around a request she'd given Jack where she'd seen no movement on his part. Beth had asked

Jack to find a recipe together, shop together and cook a gourmet dinner together. So far Jack hadn't done a thing about it.

"Is Jack a gourmet chef?" I asked.

"No."

"Does he often cook?" I wondered out loud.

I learned that Jack cooked sometimes, though it was not a passion of his. I asked if Beth she felt this was a stretch for him. She said that she had volunteered to do all of it with him so it would be easy and also a fun shared time together. While that was Beth's perspective, that may not have been Jack's. She was inviting him to participate in her area of expertise. This is analogous to a seamstress inviting her non-sewing girlfriend to sew a new dress together, where the seamstress helps her girlfriend pick out the pattern, buy the fabric and sew the garment. Fun and exciting for girlfriends. Not how guys do their lives. In the men's world this is the equivalent of an accomplished golfer inviting his non-golfing buddy to play golf, where he would set up the match, help him get clubs and then give his friend pointers while they played together in a tournament. Most men would pass on that experience.

Beyond the complexity of the request, Jack may not have been winning enough with Beth to trust that he could get a win out of this big risk. The lights were a big project and he hadn't yet gotten the win there. I suggested that Beth make sure she increases her gratitude for Jack and the small and big projects he is doing. I also reminded her that any move he makes towards fulfilling the gourmet meal request should be complimented and encouraged. For example, if Jack picks up their *Gourmet* magazine and starts looking at it, she should acknowledge and appreciate that move with him and remind him how excited she is to plan and cook the meal together. If he mentions a recipe he's heard about, or makes any passing comment that could be attributed to his working on the gourmet meal idea, he needs reinforcement via her gratitude and her enthusiasm. So often a woman is afraid to show her excitement, particularly if her man has not shown any interest in or movement towards an idea. She thinks it will put undo pressure on him. Instead, it will work in just the opposite way. Her encouragement keeps him going and reminds him of the prize: her happiness.

Part IV

Everyone Wins

Be The Change

One of my favorite quotes is "You must be the change you wish to see in the world" (Gandhi). In relationships, it is the woman's changed perspective towards her man that can make a significant difference. The good news is that women can change their viewpoint. Women grow up practicing relationships. A woman's relationship antennas are assets that help her make adjustments in all of her relationships. A woman's most successful girlfriend relationships are an example of what she has already created. Her most successful romantic relationships, however, will go beyond anything she has experienced with her girlfriends. Done well, they contain love, adoration and endless delight—bliss. That is my desire for you: relationship bliss.

There Are A Million Ways

As playful as this book is, there is a lot to take in. Some people may hit the ground running. Others will need some additional support to help get momentum behind this exciting and inspiring way of being with a man. Below are some ideas and options for how you can take this content further (and likely more will unfold over time):

♦ If you haven't already, consider reading portions of this book, or the entire book, aloud with your partner or spouse.

This will provide a good conversation starter and show where you agree or disagree. The book also offers some approaches you may decide together to explore in your relationship.

♦ Check out my website: www.CarolynCasey.net. There you can sign up for free updates about what is going on as well as register for some of the events I have listed below.

♦ Follow me on facebook for tips and ideas: www.facebook.com/carolyncaseyllc

♦ Consider taking one of the *He's Not Your Girlfriend Mini Series* workshops. To make these accessible to readers flung far and wide, these are phone events timed to consider the incredibly busy schedules and lifestyles we lead. (I also record them in case you are busier than busy and need to listen at a different time.)

In the mini series we go deeper on some of the key concepts. You will have a chance to ask questions and listen to questions others ask to make this material even more relevant to your current situation.

♦ Work with me one on one. My personal clients have concentrated and dedicated time with me to explore their unique situation, and together we travel a joy-filled path forward. If you are looking for fast and furious results, this may be the best method for you.

♦ Have me speak to your community, club or business. Let's face it, when people are happy in their love relationship, the rest of their lives flow quite beautifully. Funny how that works. I am an interactive speaker, working with the audience to help them engage with the content. Audiences leave my talks laughing, inspired and also capable of taking immediate, life-changing action.

♦ Have your book club read my book and include me, live or via phone, in your meeting. (Yes, I give discounts on my book to book clubs.) This is fun and gives you a chance, in a smaller setting and amongst friends, to learn more. I take pre-submitted questions in case anyone in the group is shy about asking around the others.

♦ Attend one of my camps. (No camping required!) These are fun and always include relationship and wisdom sessions that are life enhancing. Currently you can choose from Women's Aha! Camp or U & Me Camp. Two caveats for camp: 1) you must be female; 2) for U & Me Camp, you must bring a junior high or high school girl with you. See details on my website.

♦ Begin a regular dating practice. You will be amazed how much fun regular dates infuse in your relationship (particularly if she uses Radar Readings to help with the date ideas).

♦ Go on vacation together—just the two of you. You will experience how getting out of your regular routines opens the door for new conversation and new approaches. (Be sure to take your book with you as it's a great conversation starter.)

Visit www.CarolynCasey.net often for continually updated relationship options.

www.ingramcontent.com/pod-product-compliance
Lightning Source LLC
Chambersburg PA
CBHW072159090426
42740CB00012B/2317